GRE®EXAM*Direct*

Streamlined Review and Strategic Practice from the Leader in GRE Preparation

PUBLISHING

New York

© 2009 Kaplan, Inc.

Published by Kaplan Publishing, a division of Kaplan, Inc.
1 Liberty Plaza, 24th Floor
New York, NY 10006

Printed in the United States of America

10 9 8 7 6 5 4 3 2 1

ISBN: 978-1-60714-249-2

Kaplan Publishing books are available at special quantity discounts to use for sales promotions, employee premiums, or educational purposes. Please email our Special Sales Department to order or for more information at *kaplanpublishing@kaplan.com,* or write to Kaplan Publishing, 1 Liberty Plaza, 24th Floor, New York, NY 10006.

TABLE OF CONTENTS

kaptest.com/publishing

The material in this book is up-to-date at the time of publication. However, the Educational Testing Service may have instituted changes in the tests or test registration process after this book was published. Be sure to read carefully the materials you receive when you register for the test.

If there are any important late-breaking developments—or changes or corrections to the Kaplan test preparation materials in this book—we will post that information online at **kaptest.com/publishing.** Check to see if there is any information posted there regarding this book.

kaplansurveys.com/books

What did you think of this book? We'd love to hear your comments and suggestions. We invite you to fill out our online survey form at **kaplansurveys.com/books.**

Your feedback is extremely helpful as we continue to develop high-quality resources to meet your needs.

Part One

THE GRE

CHAPTER 1: INTRODUCTION TO THE GRE

This book will give you the info you need to conquer the Verbal and Quantitative sections on Test Day.

We know this sounds too good to be true, but we mean it. We are able to do this because we don't explain questions in isolation or focus on particular problems. Instead, we explain the underlying principles behind the Verbal and Quantitative question types on the GRE. We give you the big picture.

UNDERSTANDING THE GRE

Let's take a look at how the current GRE is constructed. As someone famous once said, "Know thine enemy." And you need to know firsthand the way this test is put together if you want to take it apart. Before you begin, though, remember that the test makers sometimes change the content, administration, and scheduling of the GRE too quickly for a published guide to keep up with. For the latest, up-to-the-minute news about the GRE, visit Kaplan's website at **kaptest.com**.

THE PURPOSES OF THE GRE

The GRE is a test that is designed to assess readiness for graduate school for a wide variety of programs. The ways in which graduate schools use GRE scores vary. Scores are often used as part of the application packet for entrance into a program, but they also can be used to grant fellowships or financial aid.

Each section of the GRE is designed to assess general skills necessary for graduate school. Some of these skills include the ability to read complex informational text and understand high-level vocabulary words in the Verbal section, the ability to respond to an issue in written form in the Analytical Writing section, and the ability to apply general mathematical concepts to a variety of problem types in the Quantitative section. Not all graduate students will find that these skills are necessary for success in their chosen programs. Nonetheless, graduate school admissions officers often view the score as an important indictor of readiness. In addition, graduate school admissions officers are comparing hundreds or even thousands of applications, and having a quantitative factor such as a GRE score makes the job of comparing so many applicants much easier. Just by purchasing this book and making a commitment to yourself to be as well prepared as possible for this exam, you've already taken the crucial first step toward making your graduate school application as competitive as possible.

THE SECRET CODE

Doing well on the GRE requires breaking down the "secret code" upon which each and every test is constructed. The GRE, like all of the tests ETS creates, is based on psychometrics, the peculiar science concerned with creating "standardized" tests. For a test to be "standardized," it must successfully do three things. First, the test must be "reliable"; in other words, a test taker who takes the GRE should get approximately the same score if he or she takes a second GRE (assuming, of course, that he or she doesn't study with Kaplan materials during the intervening period). Second—and this is closely related to our first point—it must test the same concepts on each test. Third, it must create a "bell curve" when a pool of test takers' scores are plotted; in other words, some people will do very well on the test, and some will do very poorly, but the great majority will score somewhere in the middle.

What all this boils down to is that in order to be a standardized test, the GRE has to be extremely predictable. And this is what makes the GRE and other standardized tests so coachable. Because ETS has to test the same concepts in each and every test, certain vocabulary words appear over and over again, as do variations of the same exact math questions. Moreover, the GRE has to create some questions that most test takers will get wrong—otherwise, it wouldn't be able to create its bell curve. This means that hard questions will usually contain "traps"—wrong answer choices that will be more appealing than the correct answer to a large percentage of test takers. Fortunately, these traps are predictable (this is what we mean by the secret code), and we can teach you how to recognize and avoid them. The goal of this comprehensive program is to help you break the code.

PLAY THE GAME

Too many people think of standardized tests as cruel exercises in futility, as the oppressive instruments of a faceless societal machine. People who think this way usually don't do very well on these tests.

The key discovery that people who ace standardized tests have made is that raging against the machine doesn't hurt it. If that's what you choose to do, you will just waste your energy. What these high scorers choose to do instead is to think of the test as a game—not an instrument of punishment, but an opportunity for reward. And like any game, if you play it enough times, you get really good at it.

ACQUIRE THE SKILLS

You may think that the GRE isn't a fair or decent predictor of skills—but that attitude won't help you get into graduate school.

None of the GRE experts who work at Kaplan were *born* acing the GRE. No one is. That's because these tests do not measure innate skills; they measure *acquired* skills. People who are good at standardized tests are simply people who've already acquired these skills, maybe in math class, or by reading a lot, or by studying logic in college, or perhaps the easiest way—in one of Kaplan's GRE courses. But they have, perhaps without realizing it, acquired the skills that spell success on tests like the GRE. And if *you* haven't, you have nothing whatsoever to feel bad about. You just have to acquire them now.

SAME PROBLEMS—BUT DIFFERENT

As we noted, the test makers use the same problems on every GRE. We know it sounds incredible, but it's true—only the words and numbers change. They test the same principles over and over.

Here's an example. This is a type of math problem known as a Quantitative Comparison. (Look familiar? It should, if you've ever taken an SAT. This question type used to appear on the SAT, although ETS decided to drop this question type from the SAT starting in 2005.) Your job is to examine the relationship and pick **(A)** if the term in Column A is bigger, **(B)** if the term in Column B is bigger, **(C)** if they're equal, or **(D)** if not enough information is given to solve the problem.

Column A	Column B

$$2x^2 = 32$$

x	4

Most people answer **(C)**, that they're equal. They divide both sides of the centered equation by 2 and then take the square root of both sides to get $x = 4$.

Wrong. The answer isn't **(C)**, because x doesn't have to be 4. It could be 4 *or* –4. Both work, so the answer is **(D)** because the answer cannot be determined from the information given. If you just solve for 4 you'll get this problem—and every one like it—wrong. ETS figures that if you get burned here, you'll get burned again next time. Only next time it won't be $2x^2 = 32$; it will be $y^2 = 36$ or $s^4 = 81$.

The concepts that are tested on any particular GRE—Pythagorean triangles, simple logic, word relationships, and so forth—are the underlying concepts at the heart of *every* GRE.

ETS makes changes only after testing them exhaustively. This process is called *norming,* which means taking a normal test and a changed test and administering them to a random group of students. As long as the group is large enough for the purposes of statistical validity and the students get consistent scores from one test to the next, then the revised test is just as valid and consistent as any other GRE.

That may sound technical, but norming is actually quite an easy process. We do it at Kaplan all the time—for the tests that we write for our students. While the interactive, computer-based test experience of the GRE is impossible to reproduce on paper, the paper-based test in our book is a normed exam that will produce an equivalent score.

HOW THE GRE IS ORGANIZED

The Graduate Record Examination (GRE) is administered on computer and is between two and three-quarters and three and a quarter hours long, depending on which question type you get on your experimental section (more on this in a bit). The exam consists of three scored sections, with different amounts of time allotted for you to complete each section.

Verbal	
Time	30 minutes
Length	30 multiple-choice questions
Format	Sentence Completion, Analogy, Reading Comprehension, and Antonym
Content	Tests vocabulary, verbal reasoning skills, and the ability to read complex passages with understanding and insight.

Quantitative	
Time	45 minutes
Length	28 multiple-choice questions
Format	Quantitative Comparison, Word Problems, and Data Interpretation (graph questions)
Content	Tests basic mathematical skills, ability to understand and apply mathematical concepts, and quantitative reasoning skills.

Analytical Writing	
Time	75 minutes
Length	2 essay prompts
Format	Perspective on an Issue and Analyze an Argument
Content	Tests ability to understand and analyze arguments, to understand and draw logical conclusions, and to write clearly and succinctly.

Your test will also contain an experimental section—a second Verbal or Quantitative section that the test makers put on the test so that they can norm new questions for use on future GREs. That means that if you could identify the experimental section, you could doodle for half an hour, guess in a random pattern, or daydream and still get exactly the same score on the GRE. However, the experimental section is disguised to look like a real section—there is no way to identify it. All you will really know on the day of the test is that one of the subject areas will have two sections instead of one. Naturally, many people try to figure out which section is experimental. But because ETS really wants you to try hard on it, they do their best to keep you guessing. If you guess wrong, you could blow the whole test, so we urge you to treat all test sections as scored.

After you have completed the four testlike sections, you may get a fifth "research" section, which ETS includes on the GRE to find the answers to such vital questions as how best to market its own test prep materials. The research section is unscored and is not always included in the GRE. If you see a research section on Test Day, ETS will be kind enough to tell you when it appears. So there is no reason whatsoever for you to complete it, unless you feel like doing ETS a favor or unless they offer you some reward (which they have been known to do).

SCORING

The Verbal and Quantitative sections each yield a scaled score within a range of 200 to 800. These scaled scores are like the scores that you received if you took the SAT. You cannot score higher than 800 on either section, no matter how hard you try. Similarly, it's impossible (again, no matter how hard you try) to get a score lower than 200 on either section.

But you don't receive *only* scaled scores. You will also receive a percentile rank, which will place your performance relative to those of a large sample population of other GRE takers. Percentile scores tell graduate schools just what your scaled scores are worth. For instance, even if everyone got very high scaled scores, universities would still be able to differentiate candidates by their percentile scores.

Percentile ranks match with scaled scores differently, depending on the measure. Let's imagine that you took the GRE this year and that you scored a perfect 800 on each measure type. Your scaled score would be the same in each section, but that would translate into different percentile ranks. In Verbal, you'd be scoring above 99 percent of the population, so that would be your percentile rank. But in the Quantitative section, many other people will score very high as well. Difficult as this section may seem, so many people score so well on it that high scaled scores are more common. Your percentile rank for Quantitative, even if you don't miss a single question, would be in only the 96th percentile. So many people are scoring that high in Quantitative that no one can score above the 96th percentile!

What this means is that it's pretty easy to get good scaled scores on the GRE and much harder to get good percentile ranks. A Quantitative score of 600, for example, might be okay if you're applying to a humanities program; but if you're applying to science or engineering programs, it would be a handicap at most schools. Even a score of 700 in Quantitative is relatively low for many very selective programs in the sciences or engineering—after all, it's only the 79th or 80th percentile.

The relative frequency of high scaled scores means that universities pay great attention to percentile rank. What you need to realize is that scores that seemed good to you when you took the SAT might not be all that good on the GRE. It's important that you do some real research into the programs you're thinking about. Many schools have cut-off scores below which they don't even consider applicants. But be careful! If a school tells you they look for applicants scoring 600 average per section, that doesn't mean they think those are good scores. That 600 may be the baseline. You owe it to yourself to find out what kinds of scores *impress* the schools you're interested in and work hard until you get those scores. You can definitely get there if you want to and if you work hard enough. We see it every day.

A final note about percentile rank: the sample population that you are compared against in order to determine your percentile is not everyone else who takes the test the same day you do. ETS doesn't want to penalize an unlucky candidate who takes the GRE on a date when everyone else happens to be a rocket scientist. So they compare your performance with those of a random three-year population of recent GRE test takers. Your score will not in any way be affected by the other people who take the exam on the same day as you. We often tell our students, "Your only competition in this classroom is yourself."

CANCELLATION AND MULTIPLE SCORES POLICY

Unlike many things in life, the GRE allows you a second chance. If at the end of the test, you feel that you've definitely not done as well as you can, you have the option to cancel your score. The trick is, you must decide whether you want to keep your scores before the computer shows them to you. If you cancel, your scores will be disregarded. (You also won't get to see them.) Canceling a test means that it won't be scored. It will just appear on your score report as a canceled test. No one will know how well or poorly you really did—not even you.

Two legitimate reasons to cancel your test are illness and personal circumstances that cause you to perform unusually poorly on that particular day. Also, if you feel that you didn't prepare sufficiently, then it may be acceptable to cancel your score and approach your test preparation a little more seriously the next time.

But keep in mind that test takers historically underestimate their performance, especially immediately following the test. (This underestimation is especially true on the CAT, which is designed to give you questions at the limits of your abilities.) They tend to forget about all of the things that went right and focus on everything that went wrong. So unless your performance is terribly marred by unforeseen circumstances, don't cancel your test.

If you do cancel, your future score reports will indicate that you've canceled a previous score. But since the canceled test was never scored, you don't have to worry about bad numbers showing up on any subsequent score report. If you take more than one test without canceling, then all the scores will show up on each score report, so the graduate schools will see them all. Requested score reports are sent to schools 10–15 days after the exam. All GRE testing administrations will be listed (and usable) in your ETS record for five years. Most grad schools average GRE scores, although there are a few exceptions. Check with individual schools for their policies on multiple scores.

TEST REGISTRATION

You should first obtain a copy of the *GRE Registration Bulletin*. This booklet contains information on scheduling, pricing, repeat testing, cancellation policies, and more. You can receive the booklet by calling the Educational Testing Service at (609) 771-7670 or by downloading it from **gre.org.**

The computer-based GRE General Test is offered year-round. To register for and schedule your GRE, use one of the options below. (If you live outside the United States, Canada, American Samoa, Guam, the U.S. Virgin Islands, or Puerto Rico, visit **gre.org** for instructions on how to register.)

Register Online

You can register online (if you are paying with a credit card) at **gre.org.** Once the registration process is complete, you can print out your voucher immediately (and can reprint it if it is lost).

Register by Phone

Call 1-800-GRE-CALL or 1-800-529-3590 (TTY). A confirmation number, reporting time, and test center location will be given to you when you call. Though you can register by phone up to two days before the exam, registering earlier is strongly recommended since spaces often fill quickly. Payments can be made with a Visa, MasterCard, or American Express card.

Register by Mail

Complete the Authorization Voucher Request Form found in the *GRE Registration Bulletin*. Mail the fee and signed voucher request form in the envelope provided to the address printed on the voucher.

ETS advises that you allow up to four weeks for processing before you receive your voucher in the mail. When you receive your voucher, call to schedule an appointment. Vouchers are valid for one year from the date of issue.

When you register, make sure you list a first- and second-choice test center. If you register online, you can confirm test center availability in real time.

GRE CHECKLIST

BEFORE THE TEST

- ☑ Choose a test date.
- ☑ Register online at **gre.org** or by phone at phone at 1-800-GRE-CALL.
- ☐ Receive your admission voucher.
- ☐ Check out your test center.
  - ☐ Know the kind of workstation you'll be using and whether the room is likely to be hot or cold.
  - ☐ Know the directions to the building and room where you'll be tested.
- ☐ Create a test-prep calendar to ensure that you're ready by Test Day.
  - ☐ On a calendar, block out the weeks you have to prepare for the test.
  - ☐ Based on your strengths and weaknesses, establish a detailed plan of study and select appropriate lessons and practice. (Don't forget to include some days off!)
  - ☐ Stick to the plan; as with any practice, little is gained if it isn't methodical. Skills can't be "crammed" in the last minutes.
  - ☐ Reevaluate your strengths and weaknesses from time to time and revise your plan accordingly.

THE DAY OF THE TEST

☐ Make sure you have your GRE admission voucher and acceptable ID.

☐ Leave yourself plenty of time to arrive at the test site stress-free.

☐ Arrive at the test site at least 30 minutes early for the check-in procedures.

☐ Don't stress; you're going to do great!

NAVIGATING THE GRE: COMPUTER BASICS

Let's preview the primary computer functions that you will use to move around on the GRE. The screen below is typical for an adaptive test.

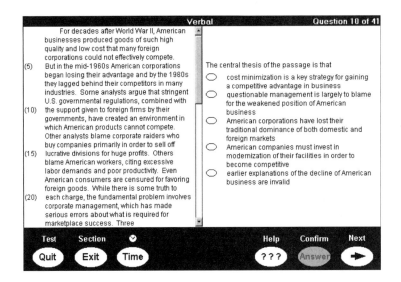

As you can see, there are empty bubbles for the answer choices—no letters (A), (B), (C), (D), (E). This is different from most multiple-choice tests.

To make the questions in this book appear as testlike as possible, the five answer choices in practice questions are not identified by letters. You will see blank ovals, just as you will on Test Day. However, for the purposes of discussion, we identify each answer choice using the corresponding letter in the answer explanation.

Here's what the various buttons do.

THE TIME BUTTON

Clicking on this button turns the time display at the top of the screen on and off. When you have five minutes left in a section, the clock flashes and the display changes from Hours/Minutes to Hours/Minutes/Seconds.

THE EXIT BUTTON

This allows you to exit the section before the time is up. If you budget your time wisely, you should never have to use this button—time will run out just as you are finishing the section.

THE HELP BUTTON

This one leads to directions and other stuff from the tutorial. You should know all this already, and besides, the test clock won't pause just because you click on Help.

THE QUIT BUTTON

Hitting this button ends the test.

THE NEXT BUTTON

Hit this when you want to move on to the next question. After you press Next, you must hit Confirm.

THE CONFIRM BUTTON

This button appears in a pop-up window after you click the Next button. The Confirm button tells the computer you are happy with your answer and are really ready to move to the next question. You cannot proceed until you have hit this button.

THE SCROLL BAR

Similar to the scroll bar on a Windows-style computer display, the scroll bar is a thin, vertical column with up and down arrows at the top and bottom. Clicking on the arrows moves you up or down the page you're reading.

PROS AND CONS OF THE COMPUTER-ADAPTIVE FORMAT

There are both good and annoying things about the GRE's computer-adaptive format. The following are a few things you should be thankful for/watch out for as you prepare to try your luck on the test.

SEVEN GOOD THINGS ABOUT THE CAT

1. There's a timer at the top of the computer screen to help you pace yourself. (You can hide it if it distracts you.)

2. There will be only a few other test takers in the room with you—it won't be like taking an exam in one of those massive lecture halls with distractions everywhere.

3. You get a one-minute pause between each section. The pause is optional, but you should always use it to relax and stretch.

4. You'll find the CAT much more convenient for your schedule than the pencil-and-paper exam. It's offered at hundreds of centers almost every day of the year.

5. Registering to take the exam is very easy, and sometimes you can sign up just a few days before you'd like to go. However, depending upon the time of the year and the availability of testing centers in your area, you may have to register several weeks in advance for a desired test date.

6. The CAT format gives you more time to spend on each question than you had on the paper-based test.

7. Perhaps the CAT's best feature is that it gives you an immediate score and your chosen schools will receive it just 20 days later.

SEVEN ANNOYING THINGS ABOUT THE CAT

1. You cannot skip around. You must answer the questions one at a time in the order the computer gives them to you. There is only one question on the screen at a time.

2. If you realize later that you answered a question incorrectly, you cannot go back and change your answer.

3. If the person next to you is noisy or distracting, the proctor cannot move you or the person, since your test is on the computer.

4. You cannot cross off an answer choice and banish it from your sight (it's on a computer screen, after all), so you have to be disciplined about not reconsidering choices you've already eliminated.

5. You have to scroll through Reading Comp passages, which means you won't be able to see the whole thing on the screen at once.

6. You can't write on your computer screen the way you can on the paper test (though some have tried), so you have to use the scratch paper they give you, which will be inconveniently located away from the computer screen.

7. Lastly, many people find that computer screens tire them and cause eyestrain—especially after four hours.

Part Two

THE VERBAL SECTION

CHAPTER 2: VOCABULARY BUILDING

INTRODUCTION TO VOCABULARY BUILDING

A strong vocabulary is the greatest asset that you can bring to the GRE Verbal section. Antonyms, which make up a quarter of the verbal section, are a direct test of your vocabulary skills. The other types of short Verbal questions (Analogies and Sentence Completions) also require you to understand the meanings of a large number of words.

This doesn't mean, however, that you should run out and memorize the dictionary. Not only is this not possible; it's not necessary. The predictability of the GRE works to your advantage. First of all, GRE Verbal tends to include a limited and predictable list of vocabulary words. Kaplan's test experts have isolated these words, and they appear in the GRE Resources section as "Top GRE Words in Context." Secondly, it is not necessary to know the exact meaning of a word to find the correct answer to an Antonym or Analogy question on the GRE. You can successfully answer most GRE Verbal questions with a rough working definition of a word rather than an exact one.

THINKING LIKE A THESAURUS

On the GRE, it is better to think like a thesaurus than like a dictionary. This means that if you think of words in groups, you will increase the bank of words that you know "close enough" and be more successful on the test. This strategy is particularly helpful for Antonym and Analogy question types.

Compare how a dictionary might define a GRE vocabulary word to how a thesaurus defines the same word:

> **Dictionary** ASSUAGE (v.): to make something less intense or severe; to satisfy or appease.
>
> **Thesaurus** ASSUAGE (v.): lessen, relieve, alleviate ameliorate, appease, mitigate, mollify, propitiate, palliate, satiate, placate, pacify, slake, quench. CALMING WORDS

If you think like a dictionary, you will know a lot about this one word. If you think like a thesaurus, you will know a little about 15 words. Let's see what this means in a testlike Antonym question.

Choose the answer choice that is most nearly opposite in meaning to the word in capital letters and then click Submit.

ASSUAGE :

○ nourish

○ restrain

● aggravate

○ delay

○ verify

Assuage means to provide relief, so its opposite would be to aggravate. If you know that *assuage* is a calming word, then you know to look for an answer meaning to agitate or make worse or more severe. Thus, **(C)** is the best response. There is no need to know the detailed dictionary definition; merely knowing that *assuage* means something similar to *calm* is enough.

By studying the word groups presented in this lesson, you can think like a thesaurus and increase your word bank quickly and efficiently.

WORD GROUPS

Here are some word groupings that can aid you in your vocabulary studies. Studying words in groups is the quickest way to bulk up your GRE vocabulary. It's a good idea to use these lists to make flashcards for studying.

These categories are *general* and not to be taken for the exact definitions of the words. Words that are in CAPS are in the Top GRE Words. All words in this list, however, have been known to appear on the GRE. (A few words with multiple meanings appear on more than one list.) An asterisk (*) means *to an excessive or negative degree.*

CALMING WORDS

alleviate, AMELIORATE, appease, ASSUAGE, lessen, mitigate, mollify, pacify, palliate, placate, propitiate, quench, relieve, satiate, slake

AGITATED

acerbate, chafe, EXACERBATE, exasperate, perturb, gall, incite, irk, nettle, peeve, perturb, pique, rile, vex

RESPECT

absolve, acclamation, accolade, adulation, AGGRANDIZE, encomium, EULOGIZE, extol, homage, kudos, LAUD, LAUDATORY, panegyric, revere, VENERATE, VENERATION

DISRESPECT

aspersion, belittle, berate, calumny, castigate, decry, defamation, denigrate, deprecate, deride, derisive, DIATRIBE, disparage, EXCORIATE, execrate, GAINSAY, HARANGUE, impudent, impugn, inculpate, inveigh, LAMBASTE, lampoon, obloquy, objurgate, OPPROBRIUM, pillory, rebuke, remonstrate, reprehend, reprove, revile, vitriolic, VITUPERATE

GOOD

affinity, altruism, amenity, amulet, auspicious, benefactor, beneficent, benign, copacetic, felicitous, humane, laudable, meritorious, munificent, philanthropy, rectitude, sacrosanct, scrupulous, seraphic

EVIL

anathema, avarice, bacchanalian, deleterious, depraved, dissipated, egregious, enormity, heinous, iniquity, invidious, libertine, libidinous, licentious, malediction, reprobate, ribald, salacious, scurrilous, sordid, TURPITUDE, virulent

TRUE

aphoristic, axiomatic, candor, candid, credence, credible, creditable, earnest, frank, incontrovertible, ingenuous, integrity, probity, unimpeachable, veracious, veracity, verisimilitude, verity, veritable

FALSE

apocryphal, blandishment, charlatan, chicanery, disingenuous, DISSEMBLE, duplicity, EQUIVOCATE, EQUIVOCATION, erroneous, ersatz, fallacious, fraudulent, guile, mendacious/mendacity, perfidious, PREVARICATE, PREVARICATION, SPECIOUS, SPURIOUS, treacherous,

HAPPINESS

animated, blithe, buoyant, content, ebullient, ecstatic, euphoric, jocular, jocund, jovial, jubilant, rapture, sanguine, vivacious

SORROW

disconsolate, doleful, dolor, elegiac, forlorn, lachrymose, lament, lamentation, lugubrious, melancholy, morose, plaintive, saturnine, threnody

CLEAR

coherent, cogent, clarity, elucidate, limpid, lucid, luculent, luminous, pellucid

UNCLEAR

abstruse, arcane, ENIGMATIC, esoteric, inscrutable, nebulous, occult, obscure, opaque, RAREFIED, RECONDITE, roiled, turbid

CLEAN

ablution, immaculate, hygienic, lavation, pristine, unsoiled, unsullied, virginal

DIRTY

besmear, besmirched, bespatter, defile, grimy, grubby, maculate, slovenly, sordid, squalid, sully

GENEROUS

altruistic, largess, MAGNANIMOUS, munificent, philanthropic, prodigal*, profligate*, spendthrift*, unstinting

GREEDY/STINGY

acquisitive, avaricious, covetous, grudging, MERCENARY, MISERLY, parsimonious, penurious, rapacious, venal

WORDY

bombastic, circumlocution, GARRULOUS, grandiloquent, LOQUACIOUS, periphrastic, prolix, turgid, voluble

TERSE

compendious, curt, epigrammatic, LACONIC, pithy, reticent, SUCCINCT, taciturn

HARMFUL

baleful, baneful, deleterious, inimical, injurious, insidious, malignant, minatory, pernicious

HEALTHFUL

invigorating, restorative, salubrious, salutary, tonic

SOOTHE

AMELIORATE, appease, ASSUAGE, MITIGATE, MOLLIFY, palliate, PLACATE, PROPITIATE, satiate, slake, quench

AGITATE

acerbate, bestir, exacerbate, exasperate, foment, gall, incite, irk, peeve, perturb, pique, rile, vex

TIMID

craven, dastardly, DIFFIDENT, pusillanimous, recreant, timorous, trepidation

BOLD

audacious, brazen*, cheek*, dauntless, effrontery*, impertinent*, impudent*, intrepid, stalwart, temerity*, undaunted

STUBBORN

IMPLACABLE, inexorable, INTRACTABLE, intransigent, OBDURATE, obstinate, pertinacious, recalcitrant, refractory, renitent, untoward, unyielding

YIELDING

amenable, compliant, docile, ductile, malleable, plastic, pliant

GROW

accrete, aggrandize, amplify, append, augment, BURGEON, escalate, upsurge, wax

SHRINK

abate, constrict, corrode, dwindle, ebb, erode, subside

INSINCERE

blandish, cajole, disingenuous, dissemble, dupe (v.), fulsome, guileful, ostensible, unctuous

SINCERE/GULLIBLE

artless, credulous, dupe (n.), guileless, ingenuous, naive

BORING

BANAL, FATUOUS, HACKNEYED, INSIPID, MUNDANE, pedestrian, PLATITUDE, prosaic, quotidian, trite

WEAKEN

ENERVATE, OBVIATE, stultify, undermine, vitiate

HOSTILE

ANTITHETICAL, bellicose, belligerent, churlish, curmudgeon, inimical, IRASCIBLE, MALEVOLENT, MISANTHROPIC, truculent, VINDICTIVE

HATRED

anathema, ANTAGONISM, ANTIPATHY, dissension, enmity, odium, rancor, repugnance

BEGINNER

callow, INCHOATE, incipient, nascent, neophyte, NOVITIATE, rudimentary, proselyte

BOSSY

authoritarian, autocrat, despotic, DOGMATIC, hegemonic, hegemony, imperious, peremptory, tyrannical

LAZY

indolent, inert, lackadaisical, languid, lassitude, lethargic, phlegmatic, QUIESCENT, slothful, torpid

FORGIVE

absolve, acquit, exculpate, EXONERATE, expiate, redress, vindicate

POOR

destitute, esurient, IMPECUNIOUS, indigent

BIASED

doctrinaire, DOGMATIC, PARTISAN, tendentious, zealot

SELFLESS

abnegate, abstemious, altruist, ASCETIC, spartan, stoic

WALKING ABOUT

ambulatory, itinerant, peripatetic

OBSTRUCT

discomfit, encumber, FETTER, forefend, hinder, impede, OCCLUDE

DISSIMILAR

ABERRANT, ANACHRONISM, ANOMALOUS, DISCRETE, HERETICAL, heterogeneous, heterodox, ICONOCLAST, MAVERICK, renegade

PLEASANT SOUNDING

consonant, dulcet, euphonious, harmonic, mellifluous, melodious, sonorous

NOISY/LOUD

cacophonous, din, discordant, dissonant, plangent, raucous

OFFENSIVE

defile, fetid, invidious, malodorous, noisome, odious, putrid, rebarbative

CONCLUSION

Remembering words in groups is great way to expand the bank of words you know "well enough" for the GRE. Spend time between now and Test Day becoming acquainted, at least superficially, with GRE vocabulary words.

The Reference section of this book provides several vocabulary-building aids, including GRE Word Groups, an extensive list of word groups that will help you "think like a thesaurus." You will also find a list of the Top GRE Words and a GRE Word Roots list. Spend some time poring through these materials and use these lists to create vocabulary flashcards, which will allow you to drill yourself on the most commonly appearing vocabulary on the GRE.

WORD GROUPS PRACTICE SET

You don't have to know the exact definition of a word to have success with GRE short verbal questions. Let's try a few exercises.

Directions: Look at the word list and decide which words deal with CLEANLINESS and which deal with DIRTINESS. Check your work in the Answers and Explanations section at the end of this lesson.

WORD	CLEAN/DIRTY
ablution	D
besmear	D
besmirched	D
bespatter	D
defile	D
grimy	D
grubby	D
immaculate	C
lavation	C
maculate	C
pristine	C
slovenly	D
sully	D
unsoiled	C
unsullied	C
virginal	C

Directions: Look at the word list and decide which words deal with GROWING and which deal with SHRINKING.

WORD	GROW/SHRINK
accrete	
abate	S
ablate	S
aggrandize	G
amplify	G

append	S
augment	G
burgeon	S
constrict	S
corrode	S
dwindle	S
ebb	S
erode	S
escalate	G
subside	S
upsurge	G
wane	S
wax	G

Directions: Look at the word list and decide which words deal with GOOD and which deal with EVIL.

WORD	GOOD/EVIL
beatific	G
beneficent	G
clement	g
continence	E
debauch	E
fiendish	E
iniquitous	e
invidious	e
lascivious	e
laudable	G
libertine	g
licentious	e
meritorious	g
miscreant	e

nefarious	g
pious	g
probity	g
rapacity	e
rectitude	g
scrupulous	g
temperance	g
turpitude	g

Directions: Look at the word list and decide which words deal with INSULTS and which deal with PRAISE.

WORD	INSULTS/PRAISE
affront	I
comment	\
decry	\
defame	\
demean	I
deride	\
derogate	\
eulogize	P
extol	P
flout	P
honor	P
laud	P
lionize	P
patronize	\
revere	P
slight	\
venerate	
vilify	

Directions: Here we have four categories. Place a check mark in the appropriate category for each word.

WORD	HAPPY	SAD	CLEVER	FOOLISH
abject			\	
astute			\	
dolorous				\
ebullient		\		
ecstatic	\			
euphoric	\			
fatuous		x		\
funereal		\		
gullible				\
inane				\
inept				\
jubilant	\			
lugubrious		\		
omniscient		\		
perspicacious				
sagacious				

ANSWERS AND EXPLANATIONS

WORD GROUPS

CLEAN	DIRTY
ablution	besmear
lavation	besmirched
immaculate	bespatter
lavation	defile
pristine	grimy
unsoiled	grubby
unsullied	maculate
virginal	slovenly
	sully

GROW	SHRINK
accrete	abate
aggrandize	ablate
amplify	constrict
append	corrode
augment	dwindle
burgeon	ebb
escalate	erode
upsurge	subside
wax	wane

GOOD	EVIL
beatific	debauch
beneficent	fiendish
clement	iniquitous
continence	invidious
laudable	lascivious
meritorious	libertine
pious	licentious

probity	miscreant
rectitude	nefarious
scrupulous	rapacity
temperance	turpitude

INSULTS	PRAISE
affront	comment
decry	eulogize
defame	extol
demean	honor
deride	laud
derogate	lionize
flout	revere
patronize	venerate
slight	
vilify	

WORD	HAPPY	SAD	CLEVER	FOOLISH
abject		✓		
astute			✓	
dolorous		✓		
ebullient	✓			
ecstatic	✓			
euphoric	✓			
fatuous				✓
funereal		✓		
gullible				✓
inane				✓
inept				✓
jubilant	✓			
lugubrious		✓		
omniscient			✓	
perspicacious			✓	
sagacious			✓	

CHAPTER 3: SENTENCE COMPLETIONS

INTRODUCTION TO SENTENCE COMPLETIONS

Sentence Completion questions constitute one-fifth of the entire Verbal section, 6 of the 30 questions. The good thing about Sentence Completions is that you can dramatically improve your performance on this question type by following a few simple rules.

The ability to follow the logic of a sentence is the main skill required for strong performance on Sentence Completions. A Sentence Completion question will present you with an incomplete sentence. Sometimes one word will be missing; sometimes two. In either case, your job is to choose the word or words that best complete the sentence.

Every Sentence Completion contains important clues—road signs or phrases—that lead you to the correct choice. Road signs are words that lead the sentence in a certain direction. Key phrases are other words that provide context and hint at the meaning of the missing word.

Let's begin by looking at a typical Sentence Completion question.

ANATOMY OF A SENTENCE COMPLETION

Here is an example of a typical Sentence Completion. This sample question includes directions, a question stem, and five answer choices.

Choose the one word or sets of words that, when inserted into the sentence, best fits the meaning of the sentence as a whole.

1. Organic farming is more labor intensive and thus initially more _____, but its long-term costs may be less than those of conventional farming.

   ⬭ uncommon

   ⬭ stylish

   ⬭ restrained

   ⊗ expensive

   ⬭ agrarian

DIRECTIONS

Take time now to familiarize yourself with the directions, as this will save you valuable time on Test Day. Sentence Completion directions ask you to find "the best" answer. This means that you should always check all the answer choices to make sure you have found the most logical completion of the sentence.

QUESTION STEM

The question stem consists of a sentence with one or more words missing. Your task is to fill in the missing words. Sentence Completion questions may feature one or two blanks. In either case, home in on the key words that provide important clues toward the logical completion of the sentence. You should pay attention, also, to the structure or pattern of the sentence.

ANSWER CHOICES

The five answer choices will consist of single words or several words that when entered into the blanks complete the sentence. Plug all the answer choices into the sentence, one by one. Don't stop when you find an answer choice that vaguely fits. Test all the choices to be sure you have found "the best" and most logical completion of the sentence.

The best answer to the sample question is (**D**) expensive.

IMPROVING SENTENCE COMPLETIONS

LOOK FOR ROAD SIGNS AND KEY PHRASES

Every Sentence Completion question provides you with important clues toward the successful completion of that sentence. The most important of these clues are "road signs." Road signs are pivotal words that indicate the direction of a sentence. Key phrases are other important words that provide context and crucial information about the correct answer.

⇐ Detour	Straight Ahead ⇒
however, although	also
instead	too
in spite of	thus
yet, but	similarly
whereas, rather	therefore
though, although	and
despite, while	likewise
on the other hand	furthermore
nevertheless	because, consequently, due to

Detour Road Signs

Detour road signs indicate that the sentence contains a contradiction or contrast. If you are on the look out for contrast, you can often predict the missing word or words (underlined in the following examples).

Example: **Despite** their cuddly looks, koala bears are actually quite ill-tempered.

Straight-ahead road signs signal that the sentence continues along in the same vein as it began. These types of sentences present a statement and supporting details.

Example: **Because** of his nefarious reputation, the politician lost the regard of voters in his district.

> **Detour road signs** indicate that the sentence contains a contradiction or contrast. If you are on the look out for contrast, you can often predict the missing word or words.
>
> **Straight-ahead road signs** signal that the sentence continues along in the same vein as it began. These types of sentences present a statement and supporting details.

Exercise—Looking for Road Signs

Directions: Find the **detour road signs** in the following sentences:

1. Male sperm whales are normally _____ creatures; however, when they are guarding their territory, they have been know to _____ ships.

2. Because the different components of the film industry were _____, it was predictable that divergent practices would arise.

3. Despite generous helpings of _____ from a group of critics, the maverick poet's three volumes have sold steadily.

4. Part of a person's _____ response to pain is determined not only by his or her emotional state but also by his or her _____ painful experience.

5. To an untrained eye, the horse appeared to be very _____, whereas in actuality, it was _____ and unmanageable.

6. Many believe that jazz improvisation is a creation of the 20th century, but improvisation may have its _____ in the figured-bass techniques of the 17th and 18th centuries.

Answers:

1. *However* is a detour road sign. This word is a clue that the sentence contains a turn in logic or presents contrasting elements.

2. This choice does not have a detour road sign. *Because* is a straight-ahead road sign. It suggests cause and effect. The sentence continues without any major reversals or contradictions.

3. *Despite* is a detour road sign. This word is a clue that the sentence contains a turn in logic or presents contrasting elements.

4. This is a tricky one, but it does not contain a detour road sign. *But also* is a straight-ahead sign, not a detour road sign. *But also* functions like *and*. *Not only* is also a straight-ahead road sign. It suggests a series of common items: *Not only this, but also that.* When evaluating road signs, use your own sense of context as the main judge of a sentence's logical direction.

5. *Whereas* is a detour road sign. This word is a clue that the sentence contains a turn in logic or presents contrasting elements.

6. *But* is a classic detour road sign. This word is a clue that the sentence contains a turn in logic or presents contrasting elements.

Key Phrases

Key phrases are the second kind of clue you will find in a sentence completion question. These words lead you to the correct answer through context. Key phrases vary depending on the sentence. Whenever you look at a Sentence Completion question, gather as many clues as you can before attempting to select an answer.

Exercise—Finding Key Phrases and Road Signs

Directions: These sentences contain both road signs and key phrases. Key phrases are **bolded.** Use the key phrases and road signs to find the correct answer.

1. Despite their **cuddly looks,** koala bears are **actually quite** _____.

   ⬭ affable

   ⬭ aggressive

2. Because of his **nefarious reputation,** the politician **lost** the _____ of voters in his district.

   ⬭ ire

   ⬭ allegiance

Answers:

1. (B)

The detour road sign *Despite* indicates you are looking for a contrast to the key phrase *cuddly looks. Aggressive* provides the contrast you need.

2. (B)

Because the politician was *nefarious,* or wicked, he lost the *allegiance,* or loyalty, of his constituents. The combination of straight-ahead road sign (*because*) and key phrase leads you to the correct answer.

SENTENCE COMPLETION WALK-THROUGH

Now let's walk you through a GRE-like Sentence Completion to demonstrate how gathering clues will help you identify the correct answer quickly and efficiently on Test Day.

SAMPLE QUESTION 1

1. The _____ of the desert explains why so many Egyptian mummies are still intact, whereas Aztec mummies have _____ in the humid tombs of the tropic rain forest.

The detour road sign *whereas* indicates that the sentence presents a contrast or change in direction. Now let's look for key phrases that also provide clues to the missing words.

The desert mummies are *intact. Desert* and *intact* are both key words that can help predict the answers.

Now that you've mined the sentence for clues, try to predict for the second blank. The road sign *whereas* indicates contrast: if the desert Egyptian mummies are intact, how might you expect to find the Aztec mummies—dehydrated or deteriorated?

The road signs and key phrases indicate that the Aztec mummies are not intact but have suffered damage in the humid environment. Therefore, *deteriorated* is a good prediction.

Now that you have mined the sentence for clues and predicted a likely answer for the second blank, go ahead and answer this sentence completion. Answers and explanations are located at the end of this section.

1. The _____ of the desert explains why so many Egyptian mummies are still intact, whereas Aztec mummies have _____ in the humid tombs of the tropical rain forest.

   ○ saturation ... petrified

   ○ altitude ... rotted

   ○ dryness ... survived

   ○ aridity ... decayed

   ○ severity ... endured

SAMPLE QUESTION 2

Try answering this Sentence Completion, paying special attention to road signs and key phrases *before* you look at the answer choices.

2. Because of his inherent _____, Dexter avoided any job that he suspected could become a travail.

   ○ impudence

   ○ insolence

   ○ eminence

   ○ indolence

   ○ imminence

SENTENCE COMPLETION TIP

Use road signs to eliminate wrong answer choices. In the following Sentence Completion from earlier in the lesson, the detour road sign *however* indicates that the first and second blank will provide contrast. Which answer choices can you eliminate based on this criterion alone?

SAMPLE QUESTION 3

3. Male sperm whales are normally _____ creatures; however, when they are jealously guarding their territory, they have been known to _____ ships.

  ○ docile ... attack

  ○ aggressive ... strike

  ○ large ... assault

  ○ peaceful ... aid

  ○ aquatic ... sink

WALK-THROUGH ANSWERS AND EXPLANATIONS

1. (D)

(D) is correct. You already knew that you wanted a word similar to *deteriorated* in the second blank. That eliminates (C) and (E). Among the remaining choices, only (D) has a word that provides a contrast to the humidity of the rain forest. Through careful gathering of clues, you could have done most of the work on this Sentence Completion *before* you even looked at the answer choices.

2. (D)

(D) is correct. The sentence begins with the straight-ahead road sign *because,* indicating that the word that fills the first blank must coincide with the meaning of the second part of the sentence. So you are looking for a descriptive term that characterizes someone who avoids *travail,* or hard work. A word similar to *lazy* would be a good prediction, and this matches up nicely with (D), *indolent.*

3. (A)

(A) is correct. The *however* road sign in the second half of this sentence indicates that a change in direction takes place. The only choice with a clear contrast between the first and second words is (A). In the second half of the sentence, the whales are "jealously guarding their territory," so you would expect a peaceful word to fit in the first blank. Only (A), *docile,* and (D), *peaceful,* work. Now you are looking for an aggressive word similar to *attack* to fit in the second blank. Of the two choices left, only (A), *attack,* works.

CONCLUSION

A good vocabulary is your greatest asset when answering Sentence Completion questions. However, paying close attention to the structural clues and key phrases within these sentences will help tremendously as well. The techniques explained in this chapter will allow you to handle such questions and make good predictions. You can usually eliminate at least some wrong answer choices on hard Sentence Completion questions, and the ability to do so will earn you points on Test Day.

SENTENCE COMPLETIONS PRACTICE SET

Try the following Sentence Completions using Kaplan's strategy above. They are more difficult than the ones you have encountered up to this point, but you should be able to handle them. Time yourself; you only have 30–45 seconds to do each question.

1. The yearly financial statement of a large corporation may seem _____ at first, but the persistent reader soon finds its pages of facts and figures easy to decipher.

   ○ bewildering

   ○ surprising

   ○ inviting

   ○ misguided

   ○ uncoordinated

2. The giant squid's massive body, adapted for deep-sea life, breaks apart in the reduced pressures of higher ocean elevations, making the search for an intact specimen one of the most _____ quests in all of marine biology.

   ○ controversial

   ○ meaningful

   ○ elusive

   ○ popular

   ○ expensive

3. Organic farming is more labor intensive and thus initially more _____, but its long-term costs may be less than those of conventional farming.

   ○ uncommon

   ○ stylish

   ○ restrained

   ○ expensive

   ○ difficult

4. Unfortunately, there are some among us who equate tolerance with immorality; they feel that the _____ of moral values in a permissive society is not only likely, but _____.

- ○ decline . . . possible
- ○ upsurge . . . predictable
- ○ disappearance . . . desirable
- ○ improvement . . . commendable
- ○ deterioration . . . inevitable

ANSWERS AND EXPLANATIONS

1. (A)

If you use the Kaplan Method, you will first look for road signs in the sentence. You should recognize the detour road sign *but,* which indicates that the correct answer will mean the opposite of how the financial statement is described at the conclusion of the sentence in the key phrase, "easy to decipher." In your own words, that opposite may be "difficult to understand." Choice (A), *bewildering,* is your answer. None of the other choices is an opposite of "easy to decipher," and can be eliminated.

2. (C)

This is a pretty straightforward Sentence Completion. The key word here is the word *intact,* which means that, although specimens have been collected, they have often (if not always) not been intact when recovered. You can fairly assert that recovering an intact specimen is difficult. When you look for a synonym for *difficult* in the answer choices, you should recognize *elusive* (C) as your answer.

3. (D)

The detour road sign in this sentence is, again, *but.* You also get a big clue with the key phrase "long-term costs" in the second half of the sentence. Your answer, *expensive* (D), is the only answer that has anything to do with costs.

4. (E)

The road signs in this question are *unfortunately* in the first half of the sentence and *not only* in the second half. *Unfortunately* tells you that the answer will match the key words "equate tolerance with immorality" and "moral values in a permissive society." Further, the second part of the road sign, *not only,* tells us that the second part of the sentence will be a continuation of the first. Paraphrasing the sentence is a good strategy here, and might sound something like this: many think being tolerant is the same thing as being immoral, so they think that the _____ of values in a society that is tolerant is not only likely but_____. A good prediction for the blanks might be "decrease" in the first blank and "certain" in the second, because those who think that tolerance is the same as immorality would think that values would decrease in a permissive society. Choice (E) is the closest match and makes sense when read into the sentence.

CHAPTER 4: ANALOGIES

INTRODUCTION TO ANALOGIES

On the GRE, you can expect to see approximately 7 Analogy questions out of the 30 questions in your 30-minute Verbal section.

While a good vocabulary is crucial when tackling GRE Verbal questions, your ability to recognize patterns between words is an important skill for success with Analogies.

All GRE Analogies are based on simple definitions. We'll show you how to use this fact to your advantage—by developing strategies you can use to answer every Analogy question, even when you don't understand all the tough vocabulary.

Let's start by looking at the structure of a typical Analogy question.

ANATOMY OF AN ANALOGY QUESTION

Following is a typical Analogy question, along with its directions.

Each of the following questions consists of a pair of words or phrases
that are separated by a colon and followed by five answer choices.
Choose the pair of words or phrases in the answer choices that are most
similar to the other pair.

MAP : ATLAS

- ⬭ key : lock
- ⬭ street : sign
- ⬭ ingredient : cookbook
- ⬭ word : dictionary
- ⬭ theory : hypothesis

DIRECTIONS

The directions tell you that Analogies are not just about vocabulary—you are dealing
with the relationships between words. On the GRE, the crux of these relationships is
how one word can be used to define the other.

STEM

The original words always have a strong relationship between them. The relationship
lies in the definition of one word in terms of the other. In this case, an *atlas* is a book
of *maps*.

ANSWER CHOICES

Of the five answer choices, only one will have the same relationship as the words in
the stem. In this case a *dictionary* is a book of *words,* just as an *atlas* is a book of *maps.*

The wrong answer choices will either have different relationships or no relationship at
all. Knowing this will allow you to eliminate incorrect answer choices and get to the
correct answer, even when you don't understand all the vocabulary.

BUILDING BRIDGES

BUILD "BRIDGES" BETWEEN THE WORD PAIRS

Analogies aren't about random associations. They test your understanding of definitions. The key to answering Analogy questions lies in forming a sentence that shows the relationship between the word pairs. This sentence is called a *bridge.*

To the test taker, there are two types of Analogy questions: the ones in which you know the meanings of both stem words and the ones in which you don't. However, many test takers who know the meanings of all the words in an Analogy question still get it wrong. This is because they rush and fall for the "trap" answer choices the test maker has set. You can avoid falling into these traps by building bridges between the stem words and plugging the answer choices into these bridges.

When you don't know the meanings of the stem words, you can often still get to the correct answer by working backward: building bridges between the answer choices and eliminating those that do not have strong relationships between the words.

Both of these techniques require that you know how to build a bridge between the paired words A bridge is a sentence that describes the relationship between the words in a word pair. The easiest way to establish this relationship is to try connecting the words in a sentence that defines one word in terms of another. In a strong bridge, you will be able to use the phrase "by definition" to describe the relationship between the words.

For example: APPLE : FRUIT

An *apple,* by definition, is a type of *fruit.*

Now try a few. For the following two questions, create a strong bridge that contains the phrase "by definition."

1. PUPPY : DOG
2. SLUGGISH : FAST

1. A *puppy,* by definition, is a *dog.* A good bridge in this case would be "A *puppy* is a young dog," or "A *puppy* is a baby *dog.*" Anything that defines a puppy in terms of the fact that it is a juvenile dog would do.

2. Something *sluggish,* by definition, is not *fast. Sluggish* means "slow moving." The stem and the correct answer choice will always have the same strong bridge between the word pairs. Keep in mind that the order of the words is important. You can build the bridge in either order, but make sure you plug the answer choices into the bridge in the same order.

STRONG AND WEAK BRIDGES

To be successful on GRE Analogy questions, it is important to learn how to make distinctions between strong and weak bridges.

1. The correct answer always has the same strong bridge as the words in the stem pair.

2. All incorrect answer choices will have either weak bridges or different bridges from the words in the stem pair.

In **strong bridges,** the word pairs are linked by strong and certain terms such as *must, are always,* and *can never.*

In **weak bridges,** the word pairs are linked by uncertain terms such as *can, should, usually,* and *may or may not.*

For example:

Strong: PRISONER : CONFINEMENT. A prisoner *by definition* is subject to confinement.

Weak: PRISONER : REFORM. A prisoner *may or may not* reform.

Confinement is an essential or defining aspect of being a *prisoner.* The bridge here is strong. On the other hand, a *prisoner* may or may not *reform.*

> **STRATEGY TIP:**
> Remember to insert *by definition* into your bridge. If your bridge still makes sense, you know you have a strong bridge.

Which one of the following word pairs has a strong bridge?

STUBBORN : YIELD ::

PEDESTRIAN : YIELD ::

By definition, someone *stubborn* refuses to *yield,* so this is a strong bridge. A *pedestrian,* however, may or may not *yield.*

Determine whether the following word pairs make strong or weak bridges. Draw an arrow from each word pair to the appropriate column.

WEAK BRIDGE		STRONG BRIDGE
	bigot : tolerance	
	bird : fly	
	bus : depot	
	butler : tact	
	hermit : solitude	
	mercenary : money	
	narration : book	
	necklace : bracelet	
	revile : dislike	
	silver : spoon	
	spinach : vegetable	
	table : chair	

Answers:

WEAK BRIDGE	STRONG BRIDGE
bird : fly	bigot : tolerance
butler : tact	bus : depot
narration : book	hermit : solitude
necklace : bracelet	mercenary : money
silver : spoon	revile : dislike
table : chair	spinach : vegetable

USING BRIDGES WHEN YOU KNOW THE VOCABULARY

Many people get Analogy questions wrong even when they know what all the words mean. This is because they don't approach the question systematically and instead go for the first answer that looks right.

Keep in mind that the stem pair and the correct answer choice will always have the same strong bridge. Approaching Analogies using the following Kaplan Method will eliminate the possibility that you will fall for tempting wrong answer choices.

THE KAPLAN 3-STEP METHOD FOR ANALOGIES

1. **Make a strong bridge between the stem words.**

2. **Go through all the answer choices and plug them into this bridge.** Eliminate any pair of words that makes no sense when plugged into this bridge.

3. **In the (rare) event that more than one answer choice works, refine your bridge by making it more specific and try it again on those answer choices.**

Step 1: Build a bridge between the stem words.

SPLINTER : WOOD ::

- ⃝ pebble : rock
- ⃝ tile : mosaic
- ⃝ water: river
- ⃝ shard : glass
- ⃝ person : crowd

Using the phrase "by definition," create a bridge between *splinter* and *wood*. The essential feature of a *splinter* is that it is a small fragment of *wood*. To keep things simple, let's just say a *splinter* is a small piece of *wood*.

Step 2: Plug this bridge into the stem words. Use the simple bridge "A *splinter* is a small piece of *wood*." Plug each of the following answer choices into this bridge. If the answer choice does not fit that bridge, eliminate it.

SPLINTER : WOOD ::

- ◯ pebble : rock
- ◯ tile : mosaic
- ◯ water : river
- ◯ shard : glass
- ◯ person : crowd

Is a *pebble,* by definition, a small piece of *rock?* A *pebble* is a small *rock,* not a small piece of *rock.*

Is a *tile,* by definition, a small piece of *mosaic?* A *mosaic* is made up of *tiles,* so a *tile* is small piece of a *mosaic.*

Is *water,* by definition, a small piece of *river?* You don't really talk about water as discrete units, so it's not quite right to say that a *water* is a small piece of a *river.*

Is a *shard,* by definition, a small piece of *glass?* Yes, a shard is a small piece of broken glass.

Is a *person,* by definition, a small piece of *crowd?* A *person* is a member of a crowd, but you wouldn't say a *person* is *by definition* a small piece of *crowd.*

Don't worry if you were unsure about which choices to eliminate. In the next step of the Kaplan Method we will refine our bridge, which will get rid of any answer choices that you were unsure about.

Step 3: If more than one answer choice works, refine your bridge and try it again on the remaining answer choices. If you weren't able to eliminate all but one of the answer choices using the simple bridge "A *splinter* is a small piece of *wood*," you could use step three, refining the bridge. What exactly is a *splinter?* A *splinter* is a small, sharp fragment of *wood*.

Plug all of the remaining answer choices into this bridge, eliminating any for which it doesn't work. This more specific bridge will help you to eliminate more answer choices.

If, for example, you were able to eliminate all of the choices except **(B)** and **(D)** in step two, you could use this more specific bridge to help you to choose the correct answer.

Is a *tile* a small, sharp fragment of a *mosaic?* A *mosaic* is made up of *tiles* that can be any shape, so a *tile* is not necessarily a small, sharp fragment of a *mosaic.*

Is a *shard* a small, sharp fragment of *glass?* A *shard* is a broken piece of *glass,* so it fits our bridge exactly. That is, a *shard* is a small, sharp, fragment of *glass.*

Now you're ready to try some Analogies practice.

ANALOGIES PRACTICE SET

Each of the following questions consists of a pair of words or phrases that are separated by a colon and followed by five answer choices. Choose the pair of words or phrases in the answer choices that are most similar to the other pair.

1. STAND : TREE ::

   ○ park : bench

   ○ academy : cadet

   ○ skein : yarn

   ○ flotilla : ship

   ○ hospital : patient

2. SODDEN : MOIST ::

   ○ maudlin : sentimental

   ○ wet : liquid

   ○ arid : harsh

   ○ nostalgic : emotional

   ○ assertive : bold

3. AUDIT : RECORDS ::

   ○ seizure : assets

   ○ violation : building

   ○ hearing : evidence

   ○ election : candidates

   ○ inventory : stock

4. CANT : SPEECH ::

   ○ dogma : belief

   ○ flattery : praise

   ○ skill : faculty

   ○ minuet : dancer

   ○ diatribe : essay

5. JUNK : SHIP ::

   ○ flower : vase

   ○ vessel : schooner

   ○ ballast : balloon

   ○ pagoda : tower

   ○ exhaust : car

6. DEHYDRATION : WATER ::

   ○ oxidation : rust

   ○ sterilization : acidity

   ○ evaporation : gas

   ○ compression : density

   ○ refinement : impurity

7. FROWARD : LED ::

   ○ contentious : argued

   ○ nugatory : overlooked

   ○ saturnine : accepted

   ✓ blasé : excited

   ○ quotidian : copied

8. INCHOATE : FORM ::

   ○ languid : vitality

   ○ diverse : harmony

   ○ spontaneous : judgment

   ○ inept : recognition

   ○ circumscribed : limit

9. FERRY : CONVEY ::

   ○ drawbridge : raise

   ○ buoy : sway

   ○ lighthouse : stand

   ○ anchor : hold

   ○ sail : furl

10. BIOLOGY : LIFE ::

   ○ zoology : zoos

   ○ astronomy : asteroids

   ○ meteorology : weather

   ○ botany : herbs

   ○ geography : maps

11. OBDURATE : RESOLUTE ::

   ○ wanton : liberal

   ○ splenetic : composed

   ○ chaste : immodest

   ○ conniving : sly

   ○ fanciful : worried

12. ETIOLATE : PALE ::

   ○ striate : grooved

   ○ cultivate : sophisticated

   ○ desiccate : drenched

   ○ enervate : excited

   ○ harden : brittle

13. HAPHAZARD : METHOD ::

   ○ boorish : behavior

   ○ random : sample

   ○ feckless : responsibility

   ○ novel : invention

   ○ moral : turpitude

14. BLEACH : HUE ::

   ○ implode: pressure

   ○ burnish : gloss

   ○ tire : energy

   ○ brace : support

   ○ blare : sound

15. CONSPICUOUS : CONCEAL ::

- ⬭ august : display
- ⬭ miserly : save
- ⬭ unhappy : cry
- ⬭ shrewd : deceive
- ⬭ bashful : embarrass

16. RULER : DISTANCE ::

- ⬭ nail : hardness
- ⬭ scale : weight
- ⬭ perfume : odor
- ⬭ truck : cargo
- ⬭ siren : sound

17. IMPORTANT : MOMENTOUS ::

- ⬭ complex : confusing
- ⬭ attractive : exquisite
- ⬭ fixed : irreparable
- ⬭ anguished : unhappy
- ⬭ concerned : determined

18. FICKLE : STABILITY ::

- ⬭ taciturn : silence
- ⬭ inflexible : rigidity
- ⬭ fidgety : nervousness
- ⬭ dogmatic : religion
- ⬭ prodigal : thrift

19. EXTORT : OBTAIN ::

- ⬭ plagiarize : borrow
- ⬭ pilfer : steal
- ⬭ explode : ignite
- ⬭ purify : strain
- ⬭ consider : appeal

ANSWERS AND EXPLANATIONS

1. (D)

By definition, a *stand* is a group of *trees*. Run through the answer choices: **(D)** is best. A *park* may or may not have *benches*. *Park bench* is a cliché trap. Therefore, you could have eliminated **(A)** even if you didn't know the words in the stem. An *academy* **(B)** is not a group of *cadets* (although *cadets* generally attend an *academy*). A *skein* **(C)** is a loosely coiled length of *yarn*, not a group of *yarn*. A *flotilla* **(D)** is a group of *ships*. A *hospital* **(E)** may have *patients*, but it is not a group of *patients*.

2. (A)

Something *sodden*, by definition, is very wet, or extremely *moist*. (This is a bridge of degree—*X* is very *Y*—a bridge that is very common on the GRE.) Something *maudlin* is, by definition, extremely *sentimental*. Therefore, **(A)** is the correct answer. Something *wet* **(B)** has *liquid* on or in it, but it is not, by definition, extremely *liquid*. You should have suspected that this was a same subject trap. Something *arid* **(C)**, meaning dry, may or may not be *harsh*. This is a weak bridge, and you could have discarded it if you didn't know the words in the stem. Something *nostalgic* **(D)**, or reminiscent of some past place or condition, may make one *emotional*, but there is no strong bridge between the two words. You could have eliminated this right off. Someone who is *assertive* **(E)**, or aggressive, may be *bold*, but there's no degree relationship here.

3. (E)

An *audit*, by definition, is a close examination of *records*. Now go through the answer choices. A *seizure* **(A)** is a confiscation of property, although not necessarily of *assets*. You could eliminate this weak bridge. A *violation* **(B)** is a finding of fault in anything, not necessarily a *building*. You could eliminate this weak bridge. A *hearing* **(C)**, or preliminary examination, may or may not contain *evidence*. You could eliminate this weak bridge. An *election* **(D)** by definition, is a choosing among *candidates*. That leaves **(E)**, and an *inventory*, by definition, is a close examination of *stock*. This is the correct answer.

4. (B)

By definition, *cant* is insincere *speech*. This is an unusual use of the word *cant*, so look at the answer choices as if you didn't understand it and see how you could have come to the answer. **(A)** *dogma*, by definition, is a doctrinaire or rigidly held *belief*. Could *cant* be doctrinaire or rigidly held *speech*? You could eliminate this unlikely bridge. **(B)** *flattery* by definition is insincere *praise*. This is likely, so keep this. **(C)** *skill* and *faculty* both mean ability, although *faculty* is more innate than *skill,* which is often learned. In any case, there is no strong bridge here, so you could eliminate this pair. A *minuet* **(D)** is a (stately, formal) dance performed by a *dancer,* so this is a strong bridge. *Cant* can't be something performed by a speech, however, so eliminate this bridge. A *diatribe* **(E)**, by definition, is a scathingly critical *essay* (although the word can also refer to speech). *Cant* could be scathing *speech*. You have now eliminated two answer choices. On Test Day, it would probably be best to not dwell on this question too much now but instead choose the best-sounding answer and move on.

5. (D)

Be on the lookout for common words with unusual meanings on the GRE. The word *junk* here refers not to garbage but to a type of ship. (It's the type seen mainly in Asian waters with sails that look like beautiful kites.) So, by definition, a *junk* is a type of *ship*. A *vase* **(A)** may be chiefly used for holding flowers, but a *ship,* most certainly, is not chiefly used for holding *junk.* **(B)** a *schooner,* or rigged ship, by definition, is a type of *vessel,* but the bridge here goes in the wrong direction. You should have been suspicious that this is a same subject trap. **(C)** *ballast* is a heavy substance used to improve the stability or control of the ascent of a *balloon* (ballast can also be used in ships). A *junk* is a type of *ship,* not something used on a *ship.* Wrong bridge. **(D)** a *pagoda,* by definition, is a type of *tower.* This is what we are looking for. **(E)** *exhaust,* by definition, is the waste produced in powering a *car,* but *junk* is not the waste produced in powering a *ship.* Wrong bridge.

6. (E)

By definition, *dehydration* is the process of removing *water.* Look for the same bridge in the answer choices. **(A)** *oxidation* is the process by which *rust* is created, not removed. **(B)** *sterilization* is the process of making infertile or of making free of microorganisms; it has nothing to do with *acidity.* You could have eliminated this weak bridge. **(C)** *evaporation* is not the process removing gas but of converting matter from liquid into *gas.* The process of *compression* **(D)** may increase *density,* but it does not remove it. **(E)** *refinement* is the process of removing *impurity,* so this is the correct answer.

7. (D)

This is a very hard question, because the vocabulary is pretty challenging. By definition, someone *froward* (meaning habitually disobedient or intractable) cannot easily be *led*. Look for this bridge in the answer choices. Although something/someone *contentious* (**A**) is likely to provoke argument, there's no strong bridge between *contentious* and *argued*. Eliminate this weak bridge. Something *nugatory* (**B**) (meaning trivial or inconsequential) is easily *overlooked*. This is a strong, but wrong, bridge. Someone *saturnine* (**C**) (meaning gloomy or sullen) may or may not be *accepted*. You could eliminate this as a weak bridge. Someone *blasé* (**D**), or jaded, cannot easily be *excited*. This is the correct bridge. Something *quotidian* (**E**) (meaning commonplace or ordinary) may or may not be *copied*. Eliminate this weak bridge.

8. (A)

By definition, something *inchoate* lacks *form*. This is another common bridge on the GRE, a bridge of lack (*X* lacks *Y*). Run this bridge through each answer choice. Something *languid* lacks *vitality*, making choice (**A**) the best answer. Things that are *diverse* (**B**) may or may not have *harmony*. Eliminate this weak bridge. Something *spontaneous* (**C**) may or may not lack *judgment*. Eliminate this weak bridge. Something *inept* (**D**) may or may not get *recognition*. Note that even if you did not know the meaning of *inchoate*, you should have been able to eliminate this and the preceding two choices for having weak bridges. By definition, something *circumscribed* (**E**) has a *limit*. However, the bridge we're looking for is *lack*. This is a strong but wrong bridge, so eliminate it.

9. (D)

The classic bridge here is *function*. The function of a *ferry* is to *convey* people, vehicles, or goods. Look for the bridge "the function of *X* is to *Y*" in the answer choices. A *drawbridge* (**A**) can be *raised*, but it would be not entirely correct to say that this was its function. The function of a *buoy* (**B**) is to mark hazards in water, or provide flotation, not to *sway*. There is no bridge here so you could have eliminated this choice. The function of a *lighthouse* (**C**) is to warn/signal navigators, not to *stand*. There is no bridge here so you could have also eliminated this one. The function of an *anchor* (**D**) is to *hold* objects in place. This is the best answer. A *sail* (**E**) function is to harness the power of the wind, not to *furl*, which is to be rolled up.

10. (C)

Biology is by definition the science or study of *life*. Look for this bridge in the answer choices. *Zoology* (**A**) is the study of all animals, not of *zoos*. *Astronomy* (**B**) is the science/study of all matter and objects in the cosmos, not just *asteroids*. *Meteorology* (**C**) is the science/study of *weather*, so this is what we are looking for. *Botany* (**D**) is by definition the science/study of all plant life, not just *herbs*. *Geography* (**E**) is the science/study of all aspects of the earth's surface, not simply *maps*.

11. (A)

This is about as tough as analogies get on the GRE. Not only is the vocabulary difficult, but the bridge between the words is quite subtle. Something *obdurate* is stubborn and hardened in wickedness. Something *resolute* is firm and unwavering. Therefore, it might initially seem like the bridge would be that something *obdurate* is, by definition, *resolute*, but that is not enough. We have to use the bridge that something *obdurate* is, by definition, *resolute* in a bad way. Look for more complicated bridges like this in the harder questions. Something *wanton* (**A**) is immoral and excessive, so something *wanton* is *liberal* in a bad way. *Splenetic* (**B**) means bad tempered and angry, so it really doesn't have much to do with being *composed*. Something *chaste* (**C**) is virtuous, while something *immodest* is vulgar, so we have a pair of antonyms here. Something *conniving* (**D**) is, by definition, *sly*. However *sly* and *conniving* both are bad, so they don't have the same bridge as the stem. Something *fanciful* (**E**) is whimsical or unreal, so it really doesn't have much to do with being *worried*.

12. (A)

This is a hard question, so the vocabulary is pretty difficult. By definition, to *etiolate* (meaning to become blanched, or make appear pale and sickly) is to make *pale*. Let's say that like most people, you didn't know what *etiolate* means. Work backward: To *striate* (**A**), meaning to mark with grooves, ribs, or stripes, is to make *grooved*. This is the correct answer. While someone *sophisticated* (**B**) is sometimes called "cultivated," there's no good bridge between *cultivate* (meaning nurture) and *sophisticated* (meaning refined or worldly). Eliminate this weak bridge. To *desiccate* (**C**), which is to dry or parch, means to make the opposite of *drenched* (meaning soaked with liquid). Do you think that *etiolate* could mean to make the opposite of *pale* (as in, to make extremely colored)? If not, then eliminate accordingly. To *enervate* (**D**), which means to sap or exhaust, is to make less *excited*. If you don't think *etiolate* could mean to make *less pale* then eliminate it. To *harden* (**E**) something may or may not make it *brittle*. Eliminate this weak bridge.

13. (C)

By definition, something *haphazard* (meaning aimless or unmethodical) lacks *method*. Try this bridge into each answer choice in turn. *Boorish* (**A**) means exhibiting rude or insensitive *behavior*, not lacking *behavior*. This is a cliché trap. While *random sample* is a common enough term, there's no good bridge between the two words, and you should eliminate (**B**). (**C**) fits perfectly: someone/something *feckless* (meaning ineffectual or irresponsible) by definition lacks *responsibility*. Something *novel* (**D**), by definition, shows *invention*, which is a strong bridge but the opposite of the bridge we want. *Moral turpitude* (**E**) is another common expression, so suspect a cliché trap. *Turpitude* means depravity, so the best bridge between the pair would be something like: *turpitude* is lacking in *moral* qualities. *Method* is lacking in *haphazard* qualities? You can eliminate this choice also.

14. (C)

By definition, to *bleach*, or to whiten, is to lose *hue*, or color. To *implode* (**A**) is to collapse inward violently. Even if you could connect *implode* with *pressure*, it's highly unlikely that you could create a useful bridge. To *burnish* (**B**) is to polish to a high *gloss*, so we have a different bridge here. To *tire* (**C**) by definition is to lose *energy*. This bridge matches. To *brace* (**D**) is to provide *support*. To *blare* (**E**) by definition is to make a loud or strong *sound*.

15. (D)

Something *conspicuous* is prominent, so, by definition, it is difficult to *conceal*. Run this bridge through the answer choices. Something *august* (**A**) is grand and stately. There is no bridge between this word and *display*, so eliminate this answer choice. Someone *miserly* (**B**) is stingy, so it makes no sense to say that he or she would be difficult to *save*. It makes no sense (and is grammatically poor) to say that someone *unhappy* (**C**) is difficult to *cry*. Someone *shrewd* (**D**) is smart, so he or she would be difficult to *deceive*. This is what you are looking for. Someone *bashful* is shy, so he or she would be easy to embarrass, and thus (**E**) is incorrect.

16. (B)

By definition, a *ruler* is used to measure *distance*. Look for the same bridge in the answer choices. A *nail* (**A**) is hard, but it doesn't measure hardness. A *scale* (**B**) is used to measure *weight*. This is the correct answer choice. *Perfume* (**C**) is a pleasing *odor*, not a measure of odor. A *truck* (**D**) carries *cargo*, but it does not measure it. A *siren* (**E**) makes a warning *sound*, but it does not measure it.

17. (B)

The bridge here is a little easier if you turn things around: something *momentous* is, by definition, very *important*. (The bridge here is one of degree, *X* is very *Y*. This is a very common bridge on the GRE.) Now plug each answer choice into the bridge, making sure you turn the choices to fit the bridge. Is something *confusing* (**A**) very *complex*? Maybe, but not always, so you can eliminate this choice. Is something *exquisite* (**B**) very *attractive*? Yes, so hold onto this. Something *irreparable* (**C**) can never be *fixed*, so eliminate this choice. Something *unhappy* (**D**) is not very *anguished*—it's the wrong way around; something *anguished* is very *unhappy*. Something *determined* (**E**) is not very *concerned*, so you can eliminate that as well. Only one answer choice worked, so there is no need to adjust the bridge here.

18. (E)

By definition, a person who is *fickle*, or changeable, lacks *stability*. This is a classic bridge of lack, another common bridge on the GRE. Plug the bridge "*X* lacks *Y*" into the answer choices. Someone who is *taciturn* (**A**) does not lack *silence*; someone who is *taciturn* is habitually not talkative. Someone *inflexible* (**B**) does not lack *rigidity;* the opposite is often true. Being *fidgety* (**C**) is often a sign of *nervousness,* so eliminate this choice, too. *Dogmatic* (**D**) means unchangeable and fixed in one's belief, so people who are *dogmatic* can lack *religion,* but certainly this is not always true. *Prodigal* (**E**) means wasteful, so someone who is *prodigal* lacks *thrift*. Only one answer choice worked, so there is no need to adjust the bridge here.

19. (A)

When you *extort* something, you obtain it by force or threats. To *extort* is to *obtain* dishonestly. If you weren't able to come up with a strong bridge initially, you might have been able to eliminate (**D**) and (**E**) at the outset by noticing that you were looking for a verb with a strong charge for the first term. Plug the bridge "*X* is to *Y* dishonestly" into the answer choices. To *plagiarize* **(A)** is to *borrow* dishonestly. Plagiarism is borrowing material from another writer without giving him or her acknowledgment. That would fit the description of borrowing dishonestly. Is to *pilfer* **(B)** to *steal* dishonestly? Well, now, this is a tricky one. *Pilfer,* which is a synonym for *steal,* is certainly dishonest, but how can you *steal* dishonestly? You can't—stealing is always dishonest—so this answer doesn't work. (By the way, answer choices that consist of pure synonyms will never be correct on the GRE.) *Explode* **(C)** is not to *ignite* dishonestly, so eliminate this choice. *Purify* **(D)** is not to *strain* dishonestly. Neither is to *consider* **(E)** to *appeal* dishonestly, so you can eliminate both of these. The bridge constructed in step one leaves only one possible answer, **(A)**.

CHAPTER 5: ANTONYMS

INTRODUCTION TO ANTONYMS

On the GRE, you can expect to see 9 or 10 Antonym questions in your 30-question, 30-minute Verbal section. This makes Antonyms the most numerous—and thus the most important—Verbal question type. Antonyms are also the most vocabulary intensive of all of the GRE Verbal question types, so it is crucial that you really focus on bolstering your vocabulary as you study.

Antonym questions are very straightforward. You are given a word, and your job is to find its opposite. It is mainly a test of your vocabulary. However, that does not mean that you have to have a huge and extensive vocabulary to do well on Antonym questions. A little strategy and some judicious guessing will often get you to the correct answer, even when you don't know all of the words involved.

Let's start by looking at the structure of a typical Antonym question.

ANATOMY OF AN ANTONYM QUESTION

Following is a typical Antonym question, along with its directions.

> **Directions:** Choose the word or phrase from the answer choices that is most nearly opposite in meaning to the capitalized word.

LAUD:

○ justify

○ educate

○ celebrate

○ eliminate

○ condemn

DIRECTIONS

The directions are straightforward—you are given a word; now find its opposite. Notice that they say the "most nearly opposite." The correct answer doesn't have to be an exact opposite but rather the best of those words you are given.

ANSWER CHOICES

The five answer choices can be either single words or short phrases. The vocabulary in the answer choices tends to be simpler than that of the stem word. Therefore, on hard Antonyms, you are more likely to know the meanings of the answer choices than that of the stem word.

ANTONYMS STRATEGIES

Ideally, you will know the meaning of the stem word and of all the answer choices for each Antonym question. However, chances are that you won't know some of the challenging vocabulary that the test maker will throw at you. If you don't know some of the vocabulary in an Antonym question, work with what you do know. If you can eliminate any of the wrong answer choices, you have a much higher chance of finding the right one by guessing strategically.

THE KAPLAN 3-STEP METHOD FOR ELIMINATING ANSWER CHOICES

1. **Eliminate answer choices that you know are wrong.** Use the answer choices by themselves to do this. You know the stem word must have a strong opposite—any answer choice that does not have a strong opposite must be incorrect.

2. **Eliminate answer choices that you think are wrong.** Use the stem word to help narrow things down. Even if you don't know exactly what a word means, you may be able to guess at its meaning from a context in which you have heard it before. Often a word will simply "sound" bad or good. Eliminate any answer choices that have the same charge as the stem word.

3. **Guess among the remaining answer choices.** Choose the strongest word—that is, the word with the most extreme meaning—from the choices that remain. Don't assume that the hardest word must be right—pick a word you know that has a strong opposite over a word you have no idea about.

Remember, however, that this is a guessing technique. It will not always lead you to the correct answer, but it will increase the odds that you guess that right answer, especially on hard questions where you don't know the meaning of the stem word.

Before we see how this technique works on some sample questions, let's take a closer look at what we mean when we say some words have no strong opposite and that some words simply sound "good" or "bad."

Identifying Words with No Opposites

Any answer choice that does not have a good opposite can be eliminated. These answer choices are always wrong. Learning how to identify words that don't have good opposites takes a little practice.

Begin by defining the word very simply before you try to find its opposite. The simpler the definition, the more likely the word will have a strong opposite. If you can't define it in a word or two, chances are it does not have a strong opposite.

Try this strategy on the following exercise.

Directions: Draw an arrow from each word to the correct column.

OPPOSITE		NO CLEAR OPPOSITE
	ascertain	
	decorate	
	deflate	
	flatter	
	hesitate	
	honor	

	loan	
	marital	
	promise	
	reject	
	represent	
	sanctify	
	triumph	

Answers:

OPPOSITE	NO CLEAR OPPOSITE
deflate	ascertain
flatter	decorate
honor	hesitate
reject	loan
sanctify	marital
triumph	promise
	represent

IDENTIFYING WORD CHARGE

Another skill that is useful in eliminating wrong answer choices is word charge—whether a word sounds "good" or "bad." You know more about words than you probably realize. Anyone who speaks English will often have a feeling about a word without necessarily being able to define it. Sometimes this is because they've heard the word used before and they have a vague sense of its meaning, even if they've never looked it up. Other times it's because words in English often sound something like their meaning. That is, "bad" words tend to be harsh and discordant sounding; for instance, *choke, besmirch,* and *noxious.* "Good" words tend to be more sonorous; that is, they just sound nicer. For example, *affluent, melodious,* and *felicity* all sound pleasant and refer to pleasant things.

On the GRE, you can use word charge to eliminate answer choices. If the stem word sounds disagreeable, eliminate the negative words in the answer choices; likewise, if the stem word sounds positive, the correct answer should be negative, so you can eliminate good-sounding words in the answer choices.

This is not a cut-and-dried technique. It will not work all of the time. However, it is certainly better than blind guessing. Take a look at the following exercise and see how good you are at identifying word charge.

Directions: Decide whether you think the following words are positive or negative. Draw an arrow from each word to the correct column.

NEGATIVE		POSITIVE
	abominate	
	acarpous	
	anathema	
	assiduous	
	beatific	
	cantankerous	
	concord	
	contentious	
	fractious	
	mendacity	
	sagacious	
	stalwart	
	untoward	

Answers:

NEGATIVE	POSITIVE
abominate	assiduous
acarpous	beatific
anathema	concord
cantankerous	sagacious
contentious	stalwart
fractious	
mendacity	
untoward	

Let's see how we can combine these techniques to eliminate answer choices in the example we saw earlier.

WHAT TO DO WHEN YOU CAN'T DEFINE THE STEM WORD

Step 1: Eliminate answer choices that you know are wrong.

Say you did not know what the word *laud* meant in the earlier example. Run through each of the answer choices and see if you can find an opposite. If you can't, you know it can be eliminated.

LAUD:

- ⬭ justify
- ⬭ educate
- ⬭ celebrate
- ⬭ eliminate
- ⬭ condemn

To *justify* is to provide a reason that something is correct. The very length of this definition would imply that there is no strong opposite.

To *educate* is to teach. There isn't really a strong opposite that means "unteach" or not to teach.

To *celebrate* is to be festive. The opposite of *celebrate* is to be sad, *mourn*.

To *eliminate* is to get rid of. The opposite of *eliminate* is *include* or *add*.

To *condemn* is to strongly disapprove. The opposite of *condemn* is *praise*.

LAUD:

- ⬭ ~~justify~~
- ⬭ ~~educate~~
- ⬭ celebrate
- ⬭ eliminate
- ⬭ condemn

Step 2: Eliminate answer choices that you think are wrong.

You can guess at the meaning of words from context, that is, where you might have heard the word. *Remember, you don't have to know the exact meaning of the word.* Merely knowing whether it means something good or something bad is sufficient to start eliminating answer choices.

Think about what *laud* might mean. Does it sound good? You may have heard something described as *laudable*. Antonyms should have opposite word charges, so eliminate any answer choice that has the same charge as the stem.

Celebrate is a positive word; it means a good thing. To *eliminate* is negative, you are wiping out something. To *condemn* is negative, you are judging something harshly.

Laud is a positive word, so we can eliminate the positive answer choice, *celebrate*.

LAUD:

○ ~~justify~~

○ ~~educate~~

○ ~~celebrate~~

○ eliminate

○ condemn

Now let's move on to the last step in the process, picking the right answer choice.

Step 3: Pick the most extreme word from the remaining choices.

Once you've done all the other eliminating you can, there's one last guessing strategy you can apply. The correct answer tends to be the strongest, most extreme word. Any word that has *very* or *extremely* as part of its definition is a good candidate.

Which do you think is more powerful a word: *eliminate* or *condemn*?

Eliminate is a negative word but not a very strong one. You talk about eliminating errors, eliminating waste, and such, all of which are quite dispassionate. To *condemn* is to be very disapproving, so it is the stronger term. Because *laud* means praise, (**E**) *condemn* is the best answer.

Let's try these steps on another question, one with phrases in the answer choices.

ELIMINATING ANSWER CHOICES WHEN THE ANSWER CHOICES ARE PHRASES

Some Antonyms have short phrases for answer choices rather than single words. Because these phrases tend to be very specific, it is often harder to find a single-word antonym for them. Consequently, the strategy of eliminating answer choices becomes much more powerful in these questions.

Most phrase answer choices are in the form of a noun with a modifying adjective or an adjective with a modifying adverb. On the GRE, the opposite is generally found by negating the modifying word. For example, in the phrase *pleasingly scented* in the following example, the opposite would be a word that means unpleasantly scented, or stinky, rather than a word that negates *scented,* such as unscented.

Other phrases, particularly ones involving verbs and adverbs, often don't have logical opposites. For instance, let's say you are given an answer choice of *agree rashly.* Would its logical opposite be agree thoughtfully, oppose rashly, or even perhaps oppose thoughtfully? A good rule of thumb is that if it takes you more than five seconds to come up with a logical opposite for an answer choice, it probably doesn't have one and you can safely eliminate it.

Bear this in mind when you try to eliminate the answer choices with no clear opposites in the following example.

Step 1. Eliminate answer choices that you know are wrong.

NOISOME:

- ◯ pleasingly scented
- ◯ marginally appealing
- ◯ persistently obstinate
- ◯ uniquely qualified
- ◯ suddenly changing

To be *pleasingly scented* is to be pleasant smelling. There are several good words that mean unpleasantly scented, such as *stinking* and *reeking.*

To be *marginally appealing* is to appeal to very few people. *Marginally* means barely. Its opposite then is *very*. There are a number of words that mean very appealing; the one that probably comes to mind first is *popular*.

To be *persistently obstinate* is to be continually stubborn. *Persistently* means almost always. Its opposite then is *rarely*. *Obstinate* means stubborn. There aren't any words that mean rarely stubborn. (Remember that you only want to negate the adjective here. A word that means never stubborn, such as *helpful*, is not an opposite.)

To be *uniquely qualified* is to be singularly fit for something. Something *unique* is one of a kind. Its opposite would be *extremely common*. There are no words that mean extremely commonly qualified, so you can eliminate this.

To be *suddenly changing* is simply that, to quickly change. A good opposite of *suddenly changing* would be a word that means slowly changing, such as *evolving*.

NOISOME:

- ⬭ pleasingly scented
- ⬭ marginally appealing
- ⬭ ~~persistently obstinate~~
- ⬭ ~~uniquely qualified~~
- ⬭ suddenly changing

Step 2: Eliminate answer choices that you think are wrong.

What do you think *noisome* might mean? Does it sound good or bad? Can you eliminate any of the following answer choices based on charge?

Pleasingly scented is a positive phrase. It means a good thing, so its opposite should be negative. If you think *noisome* is negative, do not eliminate this answer choice.

Marginally appealing is slightly negative. If you think *noisome* is also a negative word, eliminate it.

Suddenly changing is not really positive or negative; it's neutral. Because it has no charge, its opposite should also be neutrally charged. If you sense that *noisome* has a strong charge, one way or another, you can eliminate this choice.

NOISOME:

- ⬭ pleasingly scented
- ⬭ marginally appealing
- ⬭ ~~persistently obstinate~~
- ⬭ ~~uniquely qualified~~
- ⬭ suddenly changing

Now let's move on to the last step in the process, picking the right answer choice.

Step 3: Guess among the remaining answer choices.

The correct answer to a GRE Antonym question is usually the strongest, most extreme word or phrase among the answer choices. Any word that has *very* or *extremely* as part of its definition is a good candidate.

In the case of phrase answer choices, you should ask yourself which of the remaining choices—*pleasingly scented, marginally appealing,* and *suddenly changing* in this case—is likely to have the most extreme opposite. (It's almost always the choice that's the most extreme itself.) If you have to guess, choose the answer choice that has the most extreme opposite.

The opposite of *pleasingly scented* is *smelly, reeking,* or *stinking.* These are very strong words. The opposite of *marginally appealing* is *popular,* which is a fairly strong word. The opposite of *suddenly changing* is *evolving,* which is neutral. So in this case, the strongest answer is **(A)**. Because *noisome* means stinking, **(A)** is also the correct answer.

CONCLUSION

A final word about Antonyms: Sometimes you simply won't know the stem word—staring at it for a couple of minutes is not going to get you closer to the correct answer. Using word charge, word roots, and context clues, and making opposites of the answer choices can all help you, but at some point, you just have to make your best guess and move on.

A good vocabulary is your greatest asset when answering Antonym questions. However, due to the adaptive nature of the test, almost all test takers will end up seeing some words that are new to them. The techniques that you have just seen will allow you to handle such questions. You can usually eliminate at least some wrong answer choices on Antonym questions, and the ability to do so will earn you points on Test Day. Just remember the strategic approach to making an educated guess on Antonym questions.

Let's try answering a few more practice questions. All of these questions will be hard, so if you don't know the vocabulary, try eliminating answer choices.

ANTONYMS PRACTICE SET

Each question below consists of a word printed in capital letters, followed by five words or phrases. Choose the word or phrase that is most nearly opposite in meaning to the word in capital letters.

Since some of the questions require you to distinguish fine shades of meaning, be sure to consider all the choices before deciding which one is best.

1. BAWDY: *racy/lewd*

   - ☑ prudish *proper*
   - ○ superfluous *unnecessary*
   - ○ gaunt *thin*
   - ○ ethereal *heavenly*
   - ○ legitimate

2. AVER:

   - ○ move forward
   - ○ accept responsibility
   - ☑ prove false
   - ○ withhold judgment
   - ○ behave naturally

3. MEAGER: *Scant*

   - ☑ generous *plentiful*
   - ○ aggregate *grouped together*
   - ○ skeptical
   - ○ hapless *without luck*
   - ○ suave

4. DYSPHORIC: *unhappy*

   - ○ certain
   - ○ invincible
   - ☑ happy
   - ○ well-rested
   - ○ talkative

5. COGNIZANT: *to be aware*

   - ○ obsequious
   - ☑ oblivious
   - ○ vigilant
   - ○ intangible
   - ○ unwise

6. CONCISE: *brief*

   - ○ vague
   - ○ placid *calm*
   - ○ recalcitrant *stubborn/unruly*
   - ○ diverse
   - ☑ verbose

7. HUBRIS: *extreme pride*

   ○ peevish sentimentality

   ☑ humble attitude

   ○ overweening gall

   ○ concealed passion

   ○ cheerful willingness

8. DISPASSIONATE: *unbiased or objective*

   ○ sentient *aware/conscious*

   ☑ partisan *biased*

   ○ compassionate

   ○ conspicuous

   ○ heedless *reckless/neglectful*

9. ELEPHANTINE:

   ○ obese

   ○ obsolescent

   ☑ miniscule

   ○ reptilian

   ○ nuptial

10. INAUGURATE:

   ○ celebrate

   ☑ terminate

   ○ create

   ○ negate

   ○ distinguish

11. PROLIX: *wordy*

   ○ boorish

   ○ unimportant

   ☑ pithy *to the point*

   ○ diverse

   ○ disingenuous

12. REDOLENT: *pleasant smelling*

   ○ innovative

   ○ blissful

   ○ succinct

   ○ timely

   ☑ putrid

13. LAVISH:

   ☑ spartan

   ○ unsullied

   ○ venerable

   ○ besmirched

   ○ tacit

14. DISSIMILAR:

   ○ sentient *aware*

   ○ conspicuous *obvious*

   ○ truthful

   ☑ comparable

   ○ reprehensible *hateful*

15. FOE:

   ○ heretic

   ○ peer

   ✓ ally

   ○ victor

   ○ loser

16. TRANQUIL:

   ○ amenable *obedient*

   ○ disparate *different*

   ○ resilient *durable*

   ○ distinct *different*

   ✓ turbulent *restless*

17. EXTANT: *to exist*

   ○ expectant

   ○ experimental

   ✓ extinguished

   ○ extra

   ○ extrinsic

18. SEDULITY: *diligent in effort*

   ○ rejection of principles

   ○ abundance of allies

   ✓ lack of effort

   ○ openness to investigation

   ○ increase in wealth

19. CANKEROUS:

   ○ jagged

   ○ authoritarian

   ○ ornate

   ✓ uncorrupted

   ○ dangerous

ANSWERS AND EXPLANATIONS

1. (A)

Bawdy means racy or lewd. A good opposite would be *pristine* or *proper.* (**A**), *prudish,* fits perfectly. Of the wrong answers, *superfluous* means unnecessary, *gaunt* means thin, and *ethereal* means heavenly or immaterial.

2. (C)

To *aver* is to declare something forcefully or to prove it true. The opposite of this is to *prove false,* choice (**C**).

3. (A)

Meager means scant or paltry; that is, it means lacking in quantity. A word similar to *plentiful* is what you're looking for. A secondary meaning of (**A**), *generous,* is exactly that. Don't be surprised on the GRE to see common words used in slightly less than common ways. Among the wrong answer choices, *aggregate* means grouped or clustered together, to be *hapless* is to be without luck, and *suave* means sophisticated or debonair.

4. (C)

Dysphoric means displeased or unhappy. You're looking for a word that means pleased. (**C**) fits nicely. If you have trouble defining a word like this, you can look at the *dys-* prefix and expect a negative meaning to the word. Working this way, you'd guess that *dysphoric* concerned a negative or unhappy feeling, and you would choose a positive word like *happy* as your answer here.

5. (B)

To be *cognizant* is to be aware. Look for a word that means unaware. (**B**), *oblivious,* is a nice match. (**A**), *obsequious,* means overly flattering or servile. If you get stuck, try making opposites of the answer choices and comparing the opposites with the stem word. This should help you eliminate close seconds such as (**D**), *unwise.*

6. (E)

Something *concise* is brief and to the point. A good opposite would be *wordy.* This matches *verbose,* (**E**). *Recalcitrant* means stubborn or unruly. *Placid* means peaceful or calm.

7. (B)

Hubris is extreme pride or arrogance. A word such as *meekness* or *humility* would be a good bet. (B), *humble attitude,* fits the bill. Peevish means irritable, so *peevish sentimentality* is a confusing concept that is very unlikely to have clear, single-word opposite. You can get rid of (A). Likewise, (E) is rather dubious; is there a word out there that could mean *sad willingness? Overweening* means arrogant, and *gall* means nerve or effrontery—once again, a clear and logical opposite for *arrogant effrontery* does not come readily to mind. Get rid of it.

8. (B)

Someone who's *dispassionate* is unbiased or objective, so good prediction for its opposite would be biased or unfair. (B), *partisan,* meaning biased in favor of one side, matches beautifully. Of the wrong answer choices, *sentient* means conscious or aware, *conspicuous* means obvious or unsubtle, and *heedless* means reckless or neglectful.

9. (C)

Elephantine, as you may have guessed from the root word *elephant,* means extremely large. Some good synonyms are *gargantuan* or *immense.* A good prediction would be *tiny* or *small.* (C), *miniscule,* is a good match. Of the wrong answer choices, *obsolescent* means outdated. *Nuptial* means relating to weddings and marriage. If you didn't know the meaning of *minuscule,* try breaking it down some. *Minu* might remind you of words like *minute, minutia,* or *minus,* all of which have to do with smallness or brevity, making this choice your best guess. Be careful of trap answers like *reptilian* on questions like this.

10. (B)

To *inaugurate* something is to begin it. Look for a word that means end. (B), *terminate,* is right on target. If you get stuck on the meaning of a stem word such as *inaugurate,* try using clues from a context where you have heard it before. You may have heard of the inauguration of the president, which is the ceremony that marks the beginning of the president's term in office. From here, you could guess the meaning of the word and quickly locate its opposite in (B).

11. (C)

Once again, you're given a tough GRE-friendly stem word, *prolix.* If you knew that *prolix* means wordy, you could come up with the correct answer, (C), *pithy,* meaning to the point. Otherwise, once again you'd have to work with the answer choices. For instance, if you had a sense that *prolix* has a somewhat negative word charge, you'd eliminate choices that have negative word charges, **(A)**, **(B)**, and **(E)**. You could also make opposites of the answer choices; for instance, the opposite of **(D)**, *diverse,* would be *similar.* If you don't think that *prolix* means similar, you can eliminate that answer choice.

12. (E)

Something *redolent* is pleasant smelling. A good prediction would be a word such as *reeking* or *stinky.* **(E)**, *putrid,* means foul smelling and is the right choice here. *Blissful* means extremely happy. *Succinct* means concise and to the point.

13. (A)

Lavish means lush or prodigal, almost wastefully extravagant. You're looking for a choice that means sparse or unadorned. **(A)**, *spartan,* which means averse to comfort and luxury, fits nicely. *Unsullied* means untainted or pure. Conversely, *besmirched* means impure or dirty. *Venerable* means old and respectable. *Tacit* means unspoken or implied (e.g., a tacit agreement). If you're stuck, you might recall that the Spartans of ancient Greece were a rugged, harsh people. They did not indulge in lavishness in any way. Using context clues, you can sometimes glean the meaning of fairly difficult words like this.

14. (D)

Dissimilar means not similar or different. A good prediction would be *similar* or *alike.* **(D)**, *comparable,* is a good match. Of the wrong answer choices, *sentient* means conscious or aware. *Conspicuous* means obvious. *Truthful* means telling the truth, and *reprehensible* means hateful or abhorrent.

15. (C)

A *foe* is an adversary or enemy. A good prediction would be *friend.* **(C)**, *ally,* matches perfectly. A *heretic* is someone who rebels against his or her religion. A *peer* is someone of equal age or standing; he or she may be either a foe or an ally.

16. (E)

Something *tranquil* is peaceful and calm. A good opposite is *loud* or *raucous.* **(E)**, *turbulent,* which means violently agitated or restless, fits nicely. Of the wrong answer choices, *amenable* means obedient or easily led. *Disparate* and *distinct* both mean different, so neither could be correct. *Resilient* means sturdy or durable.

17. (C)

Extant means existing—so its opposite will be something that means gone or dead. (**C**), extinguished, is the best opposite. If you didn't know this, you could have eliminated answer choices that have no clear opposites. In (**A**), something *expectant* is anticipating that something will occur. (You may have heard of someone who is pregnant being referred to as *expecting.*) There is no strong opposite here. In (**B**), something *experimental* is still in the stage of being tested or has to do with being experimented upon. There is no strong opposite here. (**C**), *extinguished* means dead, so a good antonym would be *alive*. (**D**), *extra* has no strong opposite. (**E**), *extrinsic* means external or inessential. Its best opposite is *intrinsic,* which means vital or essential. *Extant* doesn't really have much of a charge, or any context clues, so go straight to step 3. *Extinguished* and *extrinsic* are about equally strong. If you have to choose between them, don't automatically go for the harder vocabulary word, *extrinsic.* In fact, if you didn't know the meaning of *extrinsic,* you should have chosen the word with a strong opposite that you did know, *extinguished.*

18. (C)

Sedulity is diligence and perseverance in labor or effort. The best antonym then is choice (**C**), *lack of effort. Sedulity* is a very hard vocabulary word, so most people will have to try to eliminate some answer choices and guess. You are working with phrases, so negate the descriptive part of the phrase when looking for an opposite.

In (**A**), the opposite of *rejection of principles* is *acceptance of principles.* Something similar to *credence* or *agreement* works as an opposite. In (**B**), the opposite to *abundance of allies* would be *lack of allies.* There does not seem to be any good one-word opposite here. In (**C**),the opposite of *lack of effort* would be *lots of effort,* so words like *industry* and *diligence* fit here. In (**D**), *openness to investigation* would have an opposite of *closed-ness to investigation,* so *evasiveness* or *secretiveness* might be an opposite here. In (**E**), *increase in wealth* has an opposite of *decrease in wealth,* so *impoverishment* might work, although it's a bit of a stretch. There is not much you can do with *sedulity* in terms of context or charge, so guess between the answer choices. When two or three answer choices are about equally strong, it usually works to go for the simplest answer choice. (**C**) might seem the most attractive. Remember, this is a guessing technique for when you don't know the vocabulary. It won't always get you to a single answer choice. However, having eliminated several wrong answer choices makes the odds of picking the right answer choice much greater.

19. (D)

Something *cankerous* is ulcerated or infected. The best antonym then is **(D)**, *uncorrupted,* which means pure and unblemished. If you did not know this, guessing might be a little tricky here. All of the answer choices have opposites, so you can't reject any of them outright in this case. (*Jagged* has an opposite in *smooth, authoritarian* has an opposite in *easygoing, ornate* has an opposite in *plain, uncorrupted* has an opposite in *corrupted,* and *dangerous* has an opposite in *safe.*) However, *cankerous* is a bad-sounding word. You also may have heard of the plant and animal disease of canker, which should be another indication that something *cankerous* is in a bad way.

So then, reject **(A)**, **(B)**, and **(E)**, all of which are either strongly or somewhat negative. That leaves you to choose between *ornate* and *uncorrupted.*

CHAPTER 6: READING COMPREHENSION

INTRODUCTION TO GRE READING COMPREHENSION

Reading Comprehension is one of four question types on the Verbal section of the GRE. It's also the most time consuming, and for many test takers the most intimidating, portion of the Verbal section. This does not have to be the case. You can expect to see two or three Reading Comprehension passages on the Verbal section, each approximately 200–300 words long and paired with two to four questions. Reading Comprehension questions comprise roughly a quarter of the entire section, about 7 or 8 out of the 30 questions you'll see.

Despite what many test takers seem to believe, Reading Comprehension questions do not test your ability to read and comprehend the passage so well that you practically memorize it. Nor do they test your ability to relate what you read to outside knowledge. Moreover, they definitely do not test your ability to offer a creative or original analysis of what you read. What Reading Comprehension questions do test is your ability to read for the gist of the passage and, where necessary, to research the passage for specific information and to select the response that best paraphrases that information.

Developing a method for handling Reading Comprehension questions quickly so that you don't get bogged down reading and rereading the passages is key to maximizing your performance on this question type. Let's begin by looking at a typical Reading Comprehension passage and question.

ANATOMY OF A READING COMPREHENSION QUESTION

Following is a typical Reading Comprehension passage and one of the questions that accompany it.

Directions: The questions in this group are based on the content of the passage. After reading the passage, choose the best answer to each question. Answer all the questions accompanying the passage on the basis of what's <u>stated</u> or <u>implied</u> in the passage.

To the historian of ideas interested in <u>examining the relationship</u> <u>between an era's scientific thought and its social milieu</u>, the late-nineteenth century "discovery" of a new radiation by the Frenchman Gustave LeBon presents a fascinating case study. LeBon, an amateur
(5) scientist, made a report in which he claimed to have found that ordinary light from an oil lamp produced invisible radiation as it impinged upon a closed metal box and that this radiation affected a photographic plate inside the box, producing an image of another plate in the box. He called this new radiation "black light" and deemed it some sort
(10) of extraordinary vibration capable of penetrating opaque objects and intermediate in nature between light and electricity.

LeBon's radiation entered the memoirs of the French Academy of Sciences alongside Roentgen's X-rays and Becquerel's uranium rays and excited vehement debate for a decade. This debate ended only
(15) after Auguste Lumière proved that the phenomenon could be produced without the intervention of light and, in fact, originated in improper chemical preparation of the plates themselves. Yet until then, the experiments and ideas of LeBon, an outsider to the universities and lycées of France, were taken quite seriously by many members of the
(20) scientific elite.

The ready acceptance of LeBon's ideas by the scientific establishment of his day was in part due to the internal upheaval in physical theory at the end of the nineteenth century. It was also assisted by his personal friendships with several members of the Academy. Most important, his
(25) success lay in his interpretation of black light, which used terminology that drew on the prevalent intellectual and philosophical trends of his time: an antirationalism and, particularly, an antimaterialism that

emphasized spontaneity, evolution, and action at the expense of the traditional emphasis in science on mechanism, determinism, and

(30)   materialism.

Which one of the following best expresses the main idea of the passage?

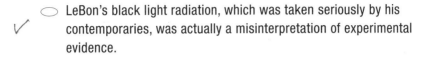 ○ LeBon's black light radiation, which was taken seriously by his contemporaries, was actually a misinterpretation of experimental evidence.

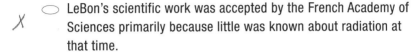 ○ LeBon's scientific work was accepted by the French Academy of Sciences primarily because little was known about radiation at that time.

✗ ○ The French Academy's acceptance of LeBon's discovery was the result of the unusually strong influence intellectuals had on the progress of science in the nineteenth century.

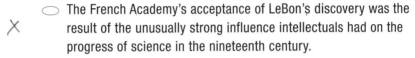 ✓ ○ LeBon's nineteenth century "discovery" of black light illustrates the ways in which culture can impact the acceptance of scientific theory.

✗ ○ The acceptance of LeBon's theories demonstrates the fact that the primary factor in the success of a scientific theory lies in its social milieu.

DIRECTIONS

There are two important facts to be gleaned from these directions. First, note that here and throughout the Verbal section, you are looking for the best answer to each question, not the right answer. In fact, the correct answer to a Reading Comprehension question tends to be fairly inconspicuous, while each of the four wrong answer choices contains something that makes it wrong. Thus, using the process of elimination is essential on this question type. Second, you must answer each question based only on what's stated or implied in the passage; applying outside knowledge can often get you into trouble.

PASSAGE

Reading Comprehension passages are written in dense, often technical prose and are adapted from books and journals in the broad areas of the humanities, the social sciences, and the natural sciences. You can expect to get at least one of each type of passage on the GRE you take. Time permitting, you are encouraged to give the passage a quick read when you first encounter it, but the focus of this reading should be on the main idea or gist of the passage, not on the mass of supporting details that the passage will invariably contain. Learning to read quickly for the gist of the passage is a skill you can acquire with just a little instruction and practice.

QUESTION

The two most common types of Reading Comprehension questions are global questions, which ask general questions about the passage, and detail questions, which require you to locate information in the passage to answer very specific questions. The question in the passage here is a global question that's asking you about the main idea of the passage, which your initial quick reading of it should reveal.

ANSWER CHOICES

One reason you don't want to spend too much time reading the passage is that you need to spend sufficient time attacking and eliminating wrong answers. Fortunately, there are ways to recognize and eliminate wrong answer choices.

READING COMPREHENSION STRATEGIES

Learn how to spend less time reading the passage and more time researching the question and attacking the answer choices.

Time management is a critical issue in Reading Comprehension. Most test takers spend far too much time reading the passage and not enough time researching the answer to the question in the passage, scrutinizing the answer choices, and choosing the best response. It's time to develop a strategic approach to Reading Comprehension.

THE KAPLAN 4-STEP METHOD FOR READING COMPREHENSION

1. **When you first encounter the passage, read enough of it to figure out the topic and the author's purpose in writing it.**

2. **Read the question.**

3. **As necessary, go back into the passage to locate the answer to the question.**

4. **Attack the answer choices and choose the one that best paraphrases the answer you found.**

READING THE PASSAGE

How you approach reading the passage may vary according to

- where you are in the Verbal section;
- whether you're running into time trouble;
- how long the passage is; and
- how difficult you find the subject matter.

Let's look at various strategies for reading the passage depending on time- and section-management issues and the difficulty of the passage.

Timing Strategies

Plan A: Lots of time/Easy passage

If it's early in the Verbal section or you know have enough time to finish the Verbal section and the passage itself doesn't present serious obstacles, do the following:

Focus on the author. GRE Reading Comprehension tests your understanding of what the author is thinking and doing. Therefore, your focus as you read must always be on the author. The test writers may want you to draw conclusions about the why and the how of the text, not the what of it—about why it has been written and how it has been put together. Focusing on authorial intent will help you better understand the passage in general—why it's organized the way it is and what the author's purpose in writing it is.

Don't sweat the details. Details are in the passage only to illustrate what the author's thinking or doing. Therefore, read over details quickly. Trying to comprehend and assimilate all of the content is a waste of time. Always boil the passage down to its basics. You can go back to find specific details as needed for the questions.

Read the first third of the passage closely. The first third of the passage is far and away the most important. Therefore, you should read it more closely than the rest of the passage because the topic and scope are revealed here, and—quite often—so are the purpose, the main idea, and the author's attitude toward the subject. Moreover, the first third provides very strong hints about the direction in which the text will go.

Note paragraph topics and make a road map (especially on longer passages). Paragraphs are the fundamental building blocks of the passage. Therefore, as you read, take note of paragraph topics and make a mental road map. Ask yourself: "What's the purpose of this paragraph? What is its basic point? How does it fit into the overall structure of the passage?" You may want to jot some notes about each paragraph on your scratch paper as you read through the passage. Creating a road map will also help you to locate relevant parts of the passage for detail questions.

> **Note:** It should not take you more than two minutes to read through the passage in this manner. At the end of this quick reading, you should be able to state in your own words the main idea of the passage.

Plan B: Not much time/Difficult passage

If it's later in the Verbal section and you have to manage your time efficiently, the passage itself is long, and/or the subject matter is difficult to get through, read the first third of passage carefully, then read the first sentence of each subsequent paragraph and the last sentence of the passage. As with all passages, focus on the gist of the passage, not the details. Apply the following reading principles:

Read with authorial intent in mind. Ask yourself, "What is the author trying to convey? Why is the passage structured as it is?"

Focus on the Big Idea(s). Even in the first third that you will be reading, focus on the big idea(s), not the supporting details.

Pay close attention to the last sentence of the passage. If you're still unsure about the main idea of the passage from the first third of the passage, pay especially close attention to the last sentence of the passage; this is where many authors tie together the loose ends and clarify the main idea of the passage.

> **Note:** This strategy is particularly useful on longer passages, particularly "hard" science passages or passages that are especially dense with details.

Take a look at the passage again, deemphasizing the sections you don't need to read.

Plan C: Very little time

If you're absolutely desperate and running into serious time trouble, you may be able to glean the main idea of the passage just by reading the first and last sentences of the passage.

> **Note:** This strategy doesn't always work and is only recommended in emergency situations. Nonetheless, if you're ever stuck trying to locate the "main idea" or "primary purpose" of a passage, these two sentences, statistically speaking, are where this information is most likely to be distilled.

Take a look at the passage again, emphasizing the sections you should focus on if you are really short on time.

ATTACKING THE QUESTIONS

Once you're familiar with the passage, you're ready to attack the questions. As mentioned, there are two broad types of GRE Reading Comprehension questions: global questions, which ask about the passage as a whole, and detail questions, which require you to locate information in the passage to answer very specific questions.

Let's examine how to attack global and detail questions, as well as a few other question types that don't fall easily into either category.

Global Questions—Main Idea

When you get a global question that asks about the main idea or primary purpose of the passage, you should not have to research the passage beyond your initial reading.

Instead, concentrate your efforts on attacking and eliminating wrong answer choices. Common wrong answer choices to global questions include those that do the following:

- Do not relate to the main idea of the passage.
- Are too specific, dealing with just one portion of the passage.
- Are too broad, going beyond the scope of the passage.
- Are too strongly worded; if an answer choice contains strong wording, ask yourself whether the wording is clearly supported by the passage. (If not, it's wrong.)
- Contradict the passage.

> **Note:** Correct answers to Reading Comprehension questions tend to have wishy-washy, qualified language. (Words such as *could, possibly, may, sometimes,* etc., are to be preferred over strong language.)

Now try to answer the following question.

Which one of the following best expresses the main idea of the passage?

○ LeBon's black light radiation, which was taken seriously by his contemporaries, was actually a misinterpretation of experimental evidence.

○ LeBon's scientific work was accepted by the French Academy of Sciences primarily because little was known about radiation at that time

○ The French Academy's acceptance of LeBon's discovery was the result of the unusually strong influence intellectuals had on the progress of science in the nineteenth century.

○ LeBon's nineteenth century "discovery" of black light illustrates the ways in which culture can impact the acceptance of scientific theory.

○ The acceptance of LeBon's theories demonstrates the fact that the primary factor in the success of a scientific theory lies in its social milieu.

(D) is the correct answer.

As is indicated by the first sentence in the passage, LeBon's "discovery" of a new radiation is of interest because it illustrates the ways in which scientific thought interacts with social milieu (i.e., the culture at large). Here's how you could have eliminated the other answer choices. **(A)** is too specific for a main-idea question; the author is not examining LeBon's "discovery" because it is a misinterpretation but because it sheds light on the ways that culture and scientific progress interact. **(B)** is also too specific for a main-idea question and is flatly contradicted by the final paragraph; lack of knowledge about radiation at the time was certainly not the primary reason for the acceptance of LeBon's theories. **(C)** again misrepresents the reasons for the acceptance of LeBon's theories, as articulated in the final paragraph. **(E)** is way too strongly worded; for instance, the passage deals with the acceptance of scientific theories, not their success.

Global Questions—Primary Purpose

Primary purpose questions are global questions that ask you to determine exactly why the author wrote this particular passage. In primary purpose questions where all the choices start with verbs, as in the following question, try a "vertical scan," looking for any verb that could disqualify an answer. As with other global questions, it's often easiest to get to the correct answer by eliminating answer choices you know are wrong.

> **Note:** If you're down to two answers, it pays to take the time to look for differences between them and, if necessary, to find something in the passage that will make one of the choices wrong.

Try the following passage and set of questions.

Congress has had numerous opportunities in recent years to reconsider the arrangements under which federal forest lands are owned and managed. New institutional structures merit development because federal forest lands cannot be efficiently managed under the
(5)   hierarchical structure that now exists.
The system is too complex to be understood by any single authority. The establishment of each forest as an independent public corporation would simplify the management structure and promote greater efficiency, control, and accountability.
(10)   To illustrate how a system for independent public corporations might work, consider the National Forest System. Each National Forest would become an independent public corporation, operating under a federal charter giving it legal authority to manage land. The charter would give the corporation the right to establish its own production goals, land
(15)   uses, management practices, and financial arrangements within the policy constraints set by the Public Corporations Board. To ensure economic efficiency in making decisions, the Public Corporations Board would establish a minimum average rate of return to be earned on assets held by each corporation. Each corporation would be required to
(20)   organize a system for reporting revenues, costs, capital investments and recovery, profits, and the other standard measures of financial health. While the financial objective would not necessarily be to maximize profit, there would be a requirement to earn at least a public-utility rate of return on the resources under the corporation's control.

(25)   Such an approach to federal land management would encourage greater efficiency in the utilization of land, capital, and labor. This approach could also promote a more stable workforce. A positive program of advancement, more flexible job classifications, professional training, and above all, the ability to counter outside bids with higher

(30)   salary would enable a corporation to retain its best workers. A third advantage to this approach is that federal land management would become less vulnerable to the politics of special interest groups.

The primary purpose of this passage is to

○ suggest that the National Forest System is plagued by many problems.

○ argue that it is necessary to restructure the management of federal forest lands.

○ insist that private corporations be allowed to manage the country's natural resources.

○ discuss the role of private corporations in the management of the National Forest System.

○ highlight the competing needs of public agencies managing national resources.

(B) is correct.

Here, the main idea of the passage is clearly found in the first paragraph: "New institutional structures merit development . . . ." The closest paraphrase of this is **(B)**, which mentions restructuring forest management.

Now let's look at the wrong answers. **(A)** is too specific and completely misses the main drift of the passage. The author mentions the problems referred to in **(A)**, but the focus is the solution, not the problems. **(C)** and **(D)** refer to private corporations—never discussed in the passage. **(E)** goes beyond the scope of the passage, referring to the competing needs of various agencies managing national resources while the passage discusses only the National Forest System.

Global Questions—Structure

Another type of global question asks about the *structure* or *organization* of the passage.

Structure questions can usually be answered by referring to your road map—the notes about the paragraphs you jotted down on the scratch paper as you read through the passage initially.

Another strategy for answering this question type is to examine the answer choices carefully, eliminating choices that contain any kind of wording that doesn't properly describe the passage.

Now try the following question.

> Which of the following best describes the organization of the passage?
>
> ✓ ○ A proposal is made, and then supporting arguments are set forth.
>
> ○ One claim is evaluated and then rejected in favor of another claim.
>
> ○ A point of view is stated, and then evidence for and against it is evaluated.
>
> ○ A problem is outlined and then various solutions are discussed.
>
> ○ Opposing opinions are introduced and then debated.

(A) is correct.

If you had created a road map by taking brief notes about the paragraphs as you read through the passage, it might have looked like this—paragraph 1: *need better forest mgmt*; paragraph 2: *how pub corps work*; and paragraph 3: *advantages*. In any case, the organization could be summarized as follows: proposed solution, detailed explanation of solution, and finally some advantages. The closest paraphrase is **(A)**, which mentions "proposal" and "support" for the proposal.

Note how each of the wrong answers has wording that makes it clearly wrong. The author evaluates a claim or proposal, as in **(B)**, but never *rejects* it for another. **(C)** is wrong because the author never gives evidence *against* the proposal. Nor does he mention other *solutions* **(D)** or *opposing opinions* **(E)**.

Detail Questions

Detail questions ask you about a specific part of the passage. On these questions, you will have to go back into the passage to research the answer.

Common wrong answer choices to detail questions include those that do the following:

- Refer to the wrong part of the passage (e.g., come from the wrong paragraph). In other words, they don't answer the question being asked.
- Use similar wording but distort what's in the passage.
- Use extreme wording.
- Contradict the passage.
- Go outside the scope of the passage, stating things that aren't said.

Let's try a detail question referring to the passage at the beginning of this chapter about Gustave LeBon.

> Which of the following is NOT given as a reason why LeBon's black light theory was accepted as reasonable?
>
> ◯ Given the knowledge of the time, it provided a plausible explanation of a reported phenomenon.
>
> ◯ It was couched in terms that reflected the prevailing inclinations in thought.
>
> ◯ It was posited at a time when arguments between scientists on the nature of radiation had not yet been settled.
>
> ✓ LeBon concealed imperfections in his method.
>
> ◯ LeBon was friends with members of the scientific establishment.

(D) is the correct answer.

> **Note:** The correct answers (or in questions like this one, the incorrect answers) to detail questions will almost always be **paraphrases** of information contained in the passage.

You're looking for the one answer that is not stated or implied in the passage. Nowhere in the passage does it say that LeBon deliberately *concealed imperfections in his method.*

In which paragraph do you expect to locate information by which to eliminate wrong answer choices? The first sentence of the final paragraph begins, "The ready acceptance of LeBon's ideas by the scientific establishment of his day was in part due to . . .," so you should read the final paragraph to answer the question.

(B) paraphrases "his success lay in his interpretation of black light, which used terminology that drew on the prevalent intellectual and philosophical trends of his time." **(C)** paraphrases the first sentence of the final paragraph, and **(E)** paraphrases the second sentence of that paragraph. **(A)** is more implied than stated; LeBon's theories would not have been taken seriously for a decade if they did not offer a plausible explanation of a reported phenomenon given the knowledge of the time.

Analogous Situation Questions

The following question is an analogous situation question; this type of question asks you to determine which answer choice describes a situation most similar to the one described in the passage. On analogous situation questions, make sure that you can put the situation or principle in your own words. Then attack the answer choices aggressively, looking for what could make an answer choice wrong.

Try the following question referring to the passage at the beginning of this chapter about Gustave LeBon.

> The acceptance of which of the following beliefs is most closely analogous to acceptance of LeBon's theories as described by the author?
>
> Although initially rejected, the genetic theories of Lysenko were forced on academics in the U.S.S.R. because of his connections within the Soviet government.
>
> Because religion placed the Earth at the center of all things, medieval scholars refused to consider other possibilities.
>
> Although based on flawed images, Lowell's claims for Martian canals gained acceptance for a time due to widespread fascination with the possibility of extraterrestrial life.

Astrology gains its authority by producing a great number of vague predictions, some of which can be interpreted as true.

 Wegener's theory of continental drift seemed initially plausible to many but only became accepted after bitter controversy over the geological evidence.

(C) is correct.

If you were to put the acceptance of LeBon's theories in your own words, you might say: His theories, although wrong, were accepted for a time primarily because they concurred with the cultural trends of his day. Likewise **(C)**, Lowell's images were flawed, but because the popular culture of his day was fascinated with the possibility of extraterrestrial life, his claims were accepted for a time.

Eliminate **(A)** because LeBon's theories, unlike those of Lysenko, were never initially rejected. Eliminate **(B)** because it doesn't discuss the acceptance of theories, merely their closed-minded rejection. **(D)** is way off and has nothing to do with LeBon's theories, and **(E)** can be eliminated because Wegener's theory was accepted eventually, unlike LeBon's theories, which were ultimately rejected.

Inference Questions

Inference questions are also quite common on Reading Comprehension. They may be either global or detail questions. Any time you are asked to determine what a passage *suggests* or what can be *inferred* from a passage, you are being asked to draw an inference, rather than find what is explicitly stated in the passage.

Don't get carried away by this distinction, however. The GRE writers never expect you to infer too much when they ask an inference question. While you may occasionally have to combine information from two parts of the passage or make a deduction, you don't want to go overboard in reading between the lines. In fact, the test maker often invites you to overthink by making a detail question look like an inference question (i.e., asking what the passage suggests when the answer is, in fact, explicitly stated).

What you need to know about this question type: The correct answer to an inference question is the one answer that **must be true** given what's stated in the passage. Consequently, common wrong answer choices on inference questions are those that do the following:

- Contradict the passage.

- Are too strongly worded.

- Go beyond the scope of the passage, suggesting things that aren't said.

Now try the following question.

> The author suggests that administrators of federal forest lands have been handicapped by which of the following?
>
> ✗ The public expectation that federal forest lands will remain undeveloped
>
> ✗ The failure of environmental experts to investigate the problems of federal forest lands
>
> ✓ The inability of the federal government to compete with private corporations for the services of skilled professionals
>
> ✗ The unwillingness of Congress to pass laws to protect federal forest lands from private developers
>
> ✗ The difficulty of persuading citizens to invest their capital in a government-run endeavor

(**C**) is correct.

Admittedly, the answer to this question is somewhat hard to locate because much of the passage talks directly or indirectly about forest management problems. Paragraph 1 mentions complexity, while paragraph 3 discusses inefficiency, personnel problems, and political issues, any of which could be the answer. (**A**), (**B**), (**D**), and (**E**) are never mentioned, while (**C**) corresponds to the personnel issue.

Line Reference Questions

Sometimes the test maker is kind enough to tell you exactly where to look in the passage to research the answer. Because you are told exactly where to go in the passage, go ahead and reread the sentence containing the line reference. Try to formulate your own answer to the question before you look at the answer choices.

The question below asks about the author's attitude. Questions that ask about the author's tone or attitude toward a subject may be either global or detail, as in this case.

Questions that ask about tone or attitude are a gift. You simply have to figure out whether the author's attitude to the subject at hand is positive or negative and eliminate answers that go the wrong way. Then get rid of answer choices that are too extreme or that are otherwise off.

> **Note:** Reading just the sentence that contains the line reference may not be sufficient; you may have to read a few lines before and after the reference to get a sense of the context.

Now try the following question.

The author's attitude toward the "hierarchical structure" mentioned in lines 4–5 can best be characterized as

- resigned.
- admiring.
- skeptical.
- bitter.
- ambivalent.

(C) is correct.

Note also that the correct answer does not require a major reach. The passage states, in reference to the proposed restructuring: "A positive program of advancement, more flexible job classifications, professional training, and above all, the ability to counter outside bids with higher salary would enable a corporation to retain its best workers." Hence, it doesn't take much inferring to conclude that present administrators are hampered by the inability to compete with private corporations for the services of skilled professionals.

CONCLUSION

As we've seen, the key to doing well on Reading Comprehension questions lies in learning how to manage your time well so that you can find the answer to the question within the passage and then attack and eliminate wrong answer choices. Make sure you practice this strategic approach to attacking Reading Comprehension questions:

1. **When you first encounter the passage, read enough of the passage to figure out the topic and the author's purpose in writing it.**

2. **Read the question.**

3. **As necessary, go back into the passage to locate the answer to the question.**

4. **Attack the answer choices and choose the one that best paraphrases the answer you found.**

Also, make sure you know the criteria by which to recognize and eliminate wrong answer choices to the various Reading Comprehension question types.

Common wrong answer choices to global questions include those that do the following:

- Do not relate to the main idea of the passage.
- Are too specific or too general.
- Are too strongly worded.
- Contradict the passage.

Common wrong answer choices to detail questions include those that do the following:

- Refer to the wrong part of the passage (don't address the question asked).
- Use similar wording but distort what's in the passage.
- Are too strongly worded.
- Contradict the passage.
- Go outside the scope of the passage, stating things that aren't said.

Common wrong answer choices on inference questions include those that do the following:

- Do not have to be true.
- Are too strongly worded.
- Contradict the passage.

READING COMPREHENSION PRACTICE SET

Directions: The questions in this group are based on the content of the passage. After reading the passage, choose the best answer to each question. Answer each question based on what's *stated* or *implied* in the passage.

Passage 1

The Gypsies, or Romani people, are found throughout Europe, as well as in the Americas, the Middle East, and Asia. A culturally linked constellation of nomadic groups, they are little understood by outsiders. Historical linguists, however, have begun to trace their migratory paths, as well as to
(5) estimate when their migrations occurred.

Most scholars agree on their basic migratory route, which began in northwestern India between 800 and 950 CE and progressed through the upper Indus Valley, across the Himalayas, and down the Silk Road to the southern shores of the Caspian Sea. From there they followed the west coast
(10) to the foothills of the Caucuses, through Armenia, and into the Byzantine Empire. The Romani then entered the Balkans and drifted throughout Europe. There is considerably less consensus, however, about whether there was one migration or several and what exactly the time frame was.

Linguists who support a single emigration hypothesis cite linguistic
(15) similarities between Romani and a group of Sanskrit-based languages that includes Rajasthani, Hindi, Gujarati, Bengali, and Multani. According to these linguists, Romani developed in parallel with these languages until the eleventh century CE and then diverged from the others, which continued to develop in synchronicity. Further, they point to the fact that all European
(20) Romani dialects include the same "loan words" from Dardic, Persian, Armenian, Byzantine Greek, Old Slavic, and Rumanian.

Other scholars, however, use linguistic evidence to show that the Romani, who today fall into three major subgroups—the Domari or *Dom*, Lomavren or *Lom*, and Romani or *Rom*—did not separate from one original group but
(25) were rather three distinct groups who left India at three different times. These researchers look to the linguistic dissimilarities among the three branches,

such as the fact that though all three branches show lexical adoption from Persian, there are no specific items shared by all three branches. Further, vestiges of a third grammatical gender in *Lom* and *Rom* indicate to these

(30)   linguists that these groups left India later than the *Dom*.

1. The author's goal in this passage could best be described as

   ○   to advocate a method for approaching the study of a specific cultural group.

   ○   to dispel a common stereotype about a specific cultural group.

   ○   to analyze a problem and offer a possible solution.

   ⊘   to describe two opinions on the history of a specific cultural group.

   ○   to explain why a traditional view is insufficient for studying a specific cultural group.

2. What is the major evidence that linguists cite to support the single-emigration hypothesis?

   ○   Similarity in language among Romani groups in geographically diverse locations

   ○   Common grammatical structures among three different branches of Gypsies

   ✓   Vocabulary found among all Romani that is borrowed from several foreign languages

   ✗   Historical records kept by the Romani indicating the path of their migration

   ✗   Consensus on the migratory path that the Romani took from India to Europe

3. Which of the following would most weaken the argument that the Romani emigrated from India at three different times?

○ Remnants of a conditional verb tense among the *Lom* not seen among the *Dom* or *Rom*

○ Variations in pronunciation of similar words among different Romani groups

○ Historical linguistic similarity between Sanskrit-based languages and the languages of other nomadic peoples following the same migratory route as the Romani

○ Archeological artifacts linking the language spoken by the Romani of the Byzantine Empire and that of modern Romani peoples

☑ Linguistic evidence that all three branches did share identical Persian words, having lost the similarity in recent centuries

Passage 2

Genetic variation is at the root of all differences found among organisms within a species. These differences determine the fitness of organisms to adapt to a changing environment—that is, to survive and live to breed and pass on their genes. This, according to Darwin's theory of evolution by natural
(5) selection, leads to the gradual evolution of the species, the famous "survival of the fittest." Therefore, analyzing how genetic changes occur is essential for understanding evolution.

While most biologists maintain that Darwin's theory is an accurate explanation for evolution of the whole organism, Motoo Kimura's work
(10) has shown that analogous processes do not dominate at the gene. Kimura's neutral theory of molecular evolution posits that, at the gene, selection follows a more haphazard pattern than might be expected, one that is largely dominated by chance. By calculating the rate of evolution in terms of nucleotide substitutions in several genes among species, Kimura noted that
(15) the substitution rate was so high that many mutations had to be selectively neutral—that is, to provide effectively no advantage or pose no barrier to the survival of an organism.

Kimura's reasoning was that so many genetic mutations exist at one time
in a population that the majority of them must exert no effect on the fitness
(20) of a species or else species would be evolving at a significantly faster rate than
is observed. Therefore, those changes that do affect the overall biology of a
species do so more likely because of chance factors that cause mutations to
be amplified and passed on.

The neutral theory does not seek to disprove the role of natural selection
(25) in mapping the road of adaptive evolution but rather complements it by
showing how the initial stages of species mutation derive not from deliberate
change but from chance. Darwin's evolutionary approach is maintained,
however, in the fact that changes that drastically reduce the survival rate
of an organism will likely not perpetuate, while those that aid survival will
(30) sustain themselves over time. Kimura colorfully contrasted his approach with
Darwin's in coining the phrase "survival of the luckiest."

4. The primary purpose of this passage is to

⊘ dispel an outdated theory by presenting new evidence.

⊘ explore the relationship between a new theory and an older, already
accepted theory.

⊘ advocate for the revision of a theory in light of new evidence.

⊘ challenge the validity of a new theory by illustrating its inability to displace
the currently accepted theory.

⊘ defend an approach to the study of a phenomenon that had previously
been dismissed as impractical.

5. What evidence would weaken Kimura's argument concerning genetic mutations as presented in the third paragraph of the passage?

   The finding that different species living in the same environment were found to have little genetic material in common

   The discovery of a species that evolves so slowly that no visible change can be seen from one generation to the next

   The discovery that almost all genetic variations affect a species' fitness, even though their impact may not be immediately visibly apparent

   The discovery that small genetic changes with little impact on survival occur more often than Kimura thought

   The finding of greater genetic variation among members of a species than had previously been noted

6. The author would be most likely to agree with which of the following statements?

   Kimura's theory negates the idea that evolution proceeds by the selective advantages and disadvantages given by variations within a species.

   New research techniques generally render older theories obsolete.

   All genetic mutations occur for specific adaptive purposes.

   Kimura's theory provides useful insight into the origins of evolutionary change before such changes can be seen.

   By only being able to theorize based on visible qualities of organisms, Darwin fell short of accurately describing evolutionary trends.

ANSWERS AND EXPLANATIONS

1. (D)

Topic and scope: The Romani and their migratory patterns; specifically, how their linguistic development may be used to trace their migrations

Author's purpose: To discuss two different hypotheses on when and how the Romani migration(s) occurred

Paragraph structure:

1. Introduces the Romanis and linguistics as a way to study their history.
2. Outlines the basic migratory route, about which most scholars agree.
3. Explains, and gives evidence for, the single-emigration hypothesis.
4. Explains, and gives evidence for, multiple emigrations.

The last sentence of the second paragraph tells us that Romani history is a subject rife with controversy. The next two paragraphs clearly present two different views of the issue, while the last paragraph further drives home the point that no one can agree on anything to do with Gypsy history. So we would be surprised if the answer took a strong stand for any one choice, thus ruling out **(A)** and **(E)**. There is no problem presented here, ruling out **(C)**, and though many stereotypes surround the Romani people, discussing them is not the main thrust of this passage, ruling out **(B)**. The correct answer, **(D)**, clearly mentions the two opinions that are presented, without taking a stand as to which is correct, exactly as the passage does.

2. (C)

The evidence for the single-emigration hypothesis will be found in **(C)**. The passage mentions linguistic similarities with other Sanskrit-based languages and "loan words" from several other languages. By looking to the passage first in this explicit text question, you will easily be able to identify the relevant information to pick **(C)** as the correct answer.

(A) is more or less true but is very nonspecific. Look for a more precise answer. **(B)** is half-right, half-wrong, because it brings in the idea of there being three branches of Gypsies, a concept espoused by the multiple-emigration folks. **(D)** not only is irrelevant, but it also misconstrues details from the passage—the Romani keep *no* historical records. **(E)** fails for similar reasons as choice **(D)**. It also misrepresents information from the passage, saying there is consensus on their migration, when the whole passage discusses the lack of consensus about their migratory past.

3. (E)

This logic question asks you to weaken the argument that the Romani emigrated from India at three different times. To weaken the argument, you will want to contest evidence or remove assumptions that would be crucial to the argument's integrity. On a difficult question like this, look carefully at where the argument is presented—in this case, in paragraph 4.

(A) should sound wrong to you, as it imagines finding more dissimilarity among different branches of Romani, which would seem to lend support to the multiple emigration hypothesis, rather than lessening its credibility. **(B)** fails for the same reasons as **(A)**, in that it offers evidence that would seem to support the argument, rather than weaken it. **(C)** is outside the scope—we don't care about other nomadic groups, only the Romani. Introducing this extraneous information just distracts us from the issue; it does nothing to the argument. You can eliminate **(D)**, as the link between modern and Byzantine-era Romani is irrelevant to the argument. **(E)** is correct because it directly undermines evidence that was used to support the multiple-emigration hypothesis.

4. (B)

Topic and scope: Motoo Kimura's neutral theory of evolution and its relationship to Darwin's theory of evolution

Author's purpose: To describe Kimura's theory and highlight how it complements Darwin's theory, creating a more complete understanding of the evolutionary process

Paragraph structure:

1. Introduces the concept of genes as the basis for evolution.

2. Presents Kimura's theory of evolution at the gene level.

3. Explains the reasoning behind Kimura's conclusions.

4. Illustrates the relationship between Kimura's and Darwin's theories and uses the phrase "survival of the luckiest" to highlight the similarities and differences between the two.

This global question asks you about the main point of the passage. You should have already done the work to answer this question by identifying the author's purpose as you read. The author is illuminating the relationship between Kimura's and Darwin's theories. This concept is conveyed by **(B)**.

(A) is wrong, because the passage clearly does not seek to dispel Darwin's theory. **(C)** does not capture the fact that Kimura came up with a new theory, not just new evidence. **(D)** also misconstrues the relationship between the two theories by suggesting that Kimura sought to disprove Darwin. **(E)** is simply off-topic, as Kimura was studying evolution through a new avenue that had never been possible before; there is no way that studying genetic variation could have been dismissed as impractical, as it was only conceived of recently.

5. (C)

This logic question asks you to weaken Kimura's argument from paragraph 3. To weaken the argument, you must first understand it and, secondly, either present counterevidence or disprove the premise underlying it. Kimura argues that because many genetic changes occur all the time *and* species do not change dramatically at a rapid rate, then most changes must not impact the fitness of a species. You will be looking for a choice that either says that genetic changes don't occur as often as Kimura thought *or* that species change more quickly than he observed. **(C)** speaks to this idea by saying that nearly all changes actually do affect the fitness of a species.

(A) goes beyond the scope of the passage by discussing variation among several different species, rather than within a given species. **(B)** supports Kimura's argument, rather than weakening it, as does choice **(D)**. **(E)** does not affect the argument in either direction, because it does not tell us whether the genetic variation translated into physical variation and differences in fitness.

6. (D)

This inference question asks you to determine which statement most closely matches the author's opinion. Neither **(A)** nor **(B)** is supported by the passage, which clearly shows that Kimura's work has complemented Darwin's, rather than rendering it obsolete. **(C)** is refuted by Kimura's research, which is detailed in paragraph 3. The main thrust of Kimura's argument is that many genetic variations serve no adaptive purpose, thus bringing into play the role of chance in producing meaningful species change. **(E)** fails because Darwin did accurately describe evolutionary trends; just because he could not explore genetic variation does not mean that he incorrectly described phenotypic (the visible characteristics of an organism) change.

(D) is correct, because it highlights the interplay between genetic and physical changes; evolution initially proceeds by chance mutations at the genetic level that appear, at first, to confer no selective advantage. To understand and measure evolutionary change fully, one must use both approaches in concert.

Part Three

THE QUANTITATIVE SECTION

CHAPTER 7: PROBLEM SOLVING

INTRODUCTION TO PROBLEM SOLVING

The 28-question Quantitative section contains about 10 Problem Solving questions, so your performance on these questions is very important to your Quantitative score.

Problem Solving questions are the classic math problems found on many standardized tests. They are standard multiple-choice math problems, consisting of a question followed by five answer choices, one of which is correct. The math tested on these questions mainly consists of junior and senior high school-level arithmetic, algebra, and geometry.

You will see that there are a variety of ways to attack Problem Solving questions later, but the first thing you need to do is familiarize yourself with this question type. Let's start by looking at a typical Problem Solving question.

ANATOMY OF A PROBLEM SOLVING QUESTION

Following is a typical Problem Solving question, along with its directions.

Directions: Solve the problem and choose the best answer.

Notes:

1. Unless otherwise indicated, the figures accompanying these questions have been drawn as accurately as possible and may be used as sources of information for answering the questions.

2. All figures lie in a plane except where noted.

3. All numbers used are real numbers.

1. A car rental company charges for mileage as follows: x dollars per mile for the first n miles and $x + 1$ dollars per mile for each mile over n miles. How much will the mileage charge be, in dollars, for a journey of d miles where $d > n$?

   ○ $d(x + 1) - n$

   ○ $xn + d$

   ⊗ $xn + d(x + 1)$

   ○ $x(n + d) + d$

   ○ $(x + 1)(d - n)$

DIRECTIONS

The directions here are straightforward.

NOTES

1. Unless otherwise indicated, the figures accompanying these questions have been drawn as accurately as possible and may be used as sources of information for answering the questions.

This means that the diagrams are accurate; you can estimate angles, lengths, and areas from them. (This question does not include any diagrams.)

2. All figures lie in a plane except where noted.

This means that the diagrams will be regular two-dimensional figures—squares, circles, and the like—unless otherwise noted.

3. All numbers used are real numbers.

This means you are not dealing with imaginary numbers such as i; that is, $\sqrt{1}$.

QUESTION

Problem Solving questions are usually pretty straightforward. They are often presented as "word problems," which present you with situations in the form of a short story and require you to conceptualize the story mathematically.

ANSWER CHOICES

Each question comes with five answer choices, only one of which is correct. If you can eliminate answer choices you know are wrong, you can home in on the correct answer or at least improve your odds of getting the question right if you have to guess.

PROBLEM SOLVING STRATEGIES

Work with the answer choices to make calculations easier.

You only get points on the GRE for getting a question right. You don't get points for your scratch work. How you arrive at the answer is immaterial.

Many people feel compelled to do Problem Solving questions the "right" way; that is, by grinding through equations the way they were forced to in junior high school. However, no one is going to give you credit for the way you approach the problem on the GRE. The right way to the answer is the fastest method that reduces your chance of error.

On every GRE question, the correct answer is right before you; you just have to work out which of the five answer choices it is. There are two alternative strategies that use this fact to help you find the answer quickly and with a minimum of messy calculation.

We call these strategies *picking numbers* and *back-solving*. Because picking numbers is generally more applicable, we'll start with it first.

PICKING NUMBERS

Take a look at the following two questions. Given the choice, which of the following would you rather solve?

Go ahead and try to solve the two questions. As you do so, think about what makes one question harder than the other.

2. Seven years from now, Carlos will be twice as old as his sister Anita will
   be then. If Carlos is now C years old, how many years old is Anita?

   $\cancel{\bigcirc}$ $\dfrac{C-7}{2}$

   $\bigcirc$ $C-7$

   $\bigcirc$ $\dfrac{C+7}{2}$

   $\bigcirc$ $\dfrac{2C-7}{2}$

   $\bigcirc$ $2C-7$

Handwritten notes:
$C = C + 7$
$A = A + 7$
$C + 7 = 2(A+7)$
$C + 7 = 2A + 14$
$C - 7 = 2A$

The answer is **(A)**.

If Carlos is now C, then in seven years he will be $C + 7$.

If Anita is now A, in seven years she will be $A + 7$.

Therefore, in seven years, $2(A + 7) = C + 7$, or $2A + 14 = C + 7$.

Solving for A we get:

$2A = C + 7 - 14 = C - 7$

So, $A = (C - 7)/2$.

2. Seven years from now, Carlos will be twice as old as his sister Anita will
   be then. If Carlos is now 13 years old, how many years old is Anita?

   $\cancel{\bigcirc}$ 3

   $\bigcirc$ 6

   $\bigcirc$ 9.5

   $\bigcirc$ 10

   $\bigcirc$ 19

Handwritten notes:
$C = 13$ now
$C + 7 = 20$
$10 - 7 = 3$
$A =$ now
$A =$ then

The correct answer is **(A)**.

If Carlos is 13 years old now, in seven years he will be 20 years old. If in seven years
Anita is half his age, she will be 10 in seven years. That is, she is now 3.

KAPLAN'S 4-STEP METHOD TO PICKING NUMBERS

1. **Pick simple numbers to stand in for the variables.**

2. **Answer the question using the number(s) you picked.**

3. **Try out all the answer choices, eliminating those that give you a different result.**

4. **Try out different values when more than one answer choice works.**

When to Pick Numbers

The first choice, **(A)**, was the correct answer to both of the previous questions. The two questions were identical, but in the second one, the variable C was replaced by the number 13, which made everything much easier to work with.

This is what picking numbers is all about, replacing confusing algebra with something much more tangible and straightforward. It's very easy to set up an equation incorrectly. By picking numbers, you needn't worry about that, and you'll know for certain that your answer is right. It's a very easy technique to learn.

There are two times when it really helps to pick numbers:

1. When there are variables in the problem and in the answer choices

2. When you are given a percent, fraction, or ratio problem with no actual values, just percentages, fractions, or ratios

Let's learn how to apply the picking numbers strategy by looking at these two cases.

Step 1: Pick simple numbers to stand in for the variables. If the answer choices contain variables or unknown values, go ahead and pick simple numbers to stand in for the variables. Make sure to note carefully on your scratch sheet what number is standing in for what variable.

Take a look at the following problem. Don't try to solve it yet.

3. If $a > 1$, what is the value of $\dfrac{2a+6}{a^2+2a-3}$?

○ a

○ $a + 3$

○ $\dfrac{2}{a-1}$

○ $\dfrac{2a}{a-3}$

○ $\dfrac{a-1}{2}$

What do you think would be a good value to pick for a? (Keep in mind that the numbers that are usually easiest to work with are small, positive integers.)

The best number to work with when picking numbers for variables is usually 2. In this case, because you are told that $a > 1$, it is the smallest positive integer you can pick.

> **Note:** In general, you should avoid picking 0 or 1 for the variable. These often cause problems when they are run through the answer choices because of their special properties.

Next let's look at what to do with our number once we have picked it.

Step 2: Answer the question using the number(s) you picked. With numbers replacing the variables, it should be easy to answer the question. The answer you come up with is your target number. It's what you're looking for in the answer choices, so circle the target number on your scratch paper before you go to the answer choices.

In the case of question 3, let's see what happens when $a = 2$:

3. If $a = 2$, what is the value of $\dfrac{2a+6}{a^2+2a-3}$?

Substitute 2 for a in the equation to answer the question:

$$\frac{2a-6}{a^2+2a-3} = \frac{2(2)+6}{(2)^2+2(2)-3} = 2$$

Therefore, when $a = 2$, the value of the expression is 2.

Step 3: Try out all the answer choices, eliminating those that give you a different result. Now try the answer choices, replacing the variables with the numbers you picked, and see if you find your target number. As soon as you see that an answer choice gives you a different result, cross it out. Make sure to try all the answer choices. Every now and then, two or more answer choices might work.

Remember, our target number is 2 when $a = 2$. Any answer choice that does not give you a value of 2 when $a = 2$ must be wrong and can be eliminated.

If $a = 2$, then . . .

(A): a is correct, so keep it.

(B): $a + 3 = 2 + 3 = 5$, so eliminate this choice.

(C): $\dfrac{2}{a-1} = 2$, so keep this choice.

(D): $\dfrac{2a}{a-3} = 4$, so eliminate it.

(E): $\dfrac{a-1}{2} = 0.5$, so eliminate it.

The only choices that yield a value of 2 when $a = 2$ are **(A)** and **(C)**.

Answer choices **(B)**, **(D)** and **(E)** do not give you a value of 2, so they cannot be right.

Step 4: Try out different values when more than one answer choice works. In the event that more than one answer choice works, simply pick different numbers and repeat the process. Don't worry about any answer choices you may have eliminated in an earlier step. Keep in mind that all of the numbers you pick must be permissible according to the problem.

Try another simple positive number for a, say $a = 3$. If we run that through the stem we get the following:

3. If $a = 3$, what is the value of $\dfrac{2a+6}{a^2+2a-3}$?

$$\frac{2a+6}{a^2+2a-3} = \frac{2(3)+6}{(3)^2+2(3)-3} = 1$$

Now you can eliminate any of the remaining answer choices that do not give you a value of 1 when $a = 3$.

- a
- ~~$a + 3$~~
- $\dfrac{2}{a-1}$
- ~~$\dfrac{2a}{a-3}$~~
- ~~$\dfrac{a-1}{2}$~~

(A) does not give you a value of 1 when $a = 3$, so it can be eliminated. That leaves **(C)** as the correct answer.

PICKING NUMBERS ON PERCENT PROBLEMS

Picking numbers is not only a great technique to use on algebra problems but also comes in handy on percent, fraction, and ratio problems where no actual values are given.

Step 1: Pick a number for the quantity in question. If you are dealing with percents, but the numerical quantities that these percents apply to are not given, you can make things a lot more concrete by picking a number to stand for those quantities.

What this means is best demonstrated by example. Take a look at the following problem. Don't try to solve it yet.

4. The value of a certain stock rose by 30 percent from March to April, then decreased by 20 percent from April to May. The stock's value in May was what percent of its value in March?

- ○ 90%
- ○ 100%
- ● 104%
- ○ 110%
- ○ 124%

Notice that even though the situation talks about the value of the stock, that value is never given. If we pick a number for the value of the stock, we can see much more easily what is going on.

Think about what would be a good number to pick for the value of the stock. (Keep in mind that you want a number that it is easy to find percentages of.)

The best number to pick when dealing with percents is almost always 100. It is very easy to find any percentage of 100.

Step 2: Answer the question using the number you picked. Apply the percents in the question stem to the number you picked.

In the case of question 4, let's see what happens when the stock's value is 100:

4. The value of a certain stock rose by 30 percent from March to April, then decreased by 20 percent from April to May. The stock's value in May was what percent of its value in March?

Apply the percent changes to 100.

Thirty percent of 100 is 30. Therefore, if the stock's value rises by 30 percent, its new value is 130.

Next, decrease this number by 20 percent.

Twenty percent of 130 is $0.20 \times 130 = 26$. So a decrease in price of 20 percent is $130 - 26 = 104$.

Step 3: Look for your target value in the answer choices. The original value was 100, and the new value is 104. So the stock is 104 percent of its original value. That's **(C)**.

> The value of a certain stock rose by 30 percent from March to April, then decreased by 20 percent from April to May. The stock's value in May was what percent of its value in March?
>
> ○ 90%
>
> ○ 100%
>
> ● 104%
>
> ○ 110%
>
> ○ 124%

Now try picking numbers on the following questions.

PICKING NUMBERS PRACTICE

As you've already seen, sometimes you may have to pick more than one number. This shouldn't cause any problems, as long as the numbers you pick are easy to work with.

Don't try to make the numbers realistic; for instance, in the following question, you should not make the charge for mileage 0.25 dollars per mile for the first 200 miles.

> 5. A car rental company charges for mileage as follows: x dollars per mile for the first n miles and $x + 1$ dollars per mile for each mile over n miles. How much will the mileage charge be in dollars for a journey of d miles where $d > n$?
>
> ○ $d(x + 1) - n$
>
> ○ $xn + d$
>
> ○ $xn + d(x + 1)$
>
> ○ $x(n + d) + d$
>
> ○ $(x + 1)(d - n)$

You've seen how picking 100 works for attacking percent problems; you also want to pick numbers on fraction and ratio problems where no actual values are given. In the problem below, because no actual numbers are given, you can go ahead and pick a number that works well with the fractions in the problem to represent the number of people at the function. This will make everything a lot more concrete. Check out the denominators of the answer choices when choosing your number on fraction questions. In most cases, the largest common denominator among your answer choices is a good selection.

6. At a certain international function, $\frac{1}{5}$ of the people attending were male Greek citizens. If the number of female Greek citizens attending was $\frac{2}{3}$ greater than the number of male Greek citizens attending, what fraction of the people at the dinner were not Greek citizens?

    ○ $\frac{1}{5}$

    ○ $\frac{2}{5}$

    ○ $\frac{7}{15}$

    ○ $\frac{8}{15}$

    ○ $\frac{2}{3}$

BACK-SOLVING

Back-solving is another strategy that allows you to solve complicated equations quickly. Remember, the right answer to any GRE question is always there before you, and you can use this fact to solve equations.

Look at the following question. It contains a very complicated equation, one that you would probably not want to solve algebraically on Test Day. However, it becomes much easier to work with if you realize that only one answer choice is right; that is, only one answer choice will give you a value of 0 when plugged into the equation.

7. What is the value of x if $\dfrac{x+1}{x-3} - \dfrac{x+2}{x-4} = 0$?

- ⭘ −2
- ⭘ −1
- ⭘ 0
- ⭘ 1
- ⭘ 2

Plug the answer choices into the equation. The one that gives you 0 must be correct.

(C): $\dfrac{x+1}{x-3} - \dfrac{x+2}{x-4} = \dfrac{0+1}{0-3} - \dfrac{0+2}{0-4} = \dfrac{1}{-3} - \dfrac{2}{-4} \neq 0$. Eliminate this answer choice.

Try another answer choice, one that is easy to work with.

(D): $\dfrac{x+1}{x-3} - \dfrac{x+2}{x-4} = \dfrac{1+1}{1-3} - \dfrac{1+2}{1-4} = \dfrac{2}{-2} - \dfrac{3}{-3} = -1 - (-1) = 0$. Because the equation is true for **(D)**, it must be the answer.

When back-solving, once you find an answer choice that works, stop working on that question, choose that answer choice, and move on.

On the GRE, many equation problems are not written in mathematical terms but are presented as word problems. Back-solving works great for these problems—you don't even need to translate the question stem into math (which is where most errors occur).

Let's try an example. Take a quick look at the following question stem and ask yourself exactly what it is you're trying to find.

8. Employee X is paid $12.50 an hour no matter how many hours he works per week. Employee Y is paid $10 an hour for the first 30 hours she works in a week and is paid 1.5 times that for every hour over that. On a certain week, both employees worked the same number of hours and were paid the same amount. How many hours did each employee work that week?

- ⬭ 48
- ⬭ 50
- ⬭ 54
- ⬭ 60
- ⬭ 64

Start with **(C)** because most questions with numbers in the answer choices are arranged in ascending order. If **(C)** doesn't work, you can often tell whether it is too small or too large. In that case you can eliminate other answer choices that are smaller or larger.

In 54 hours, employee X earns 54 × $12.50 = $675.

In 54 hours, employee Y earns 30 × $10 + 24 × 15 = $660.

Because these quantities are not equal, **(C)** is not correct.

Bearing all of this in mind, let's check out the remaining answer choices.

Employee X earns more than employee Y for the first 30 hours but less than employee Y after that. If they work long enough, employee Y's earnings will catch up to and overtake those of employee X.

If they both work 54 hours, employee Y earns less than employee X. For their earnings to be equal, they will have to work still more hours. Therefore, you can eliminate **(C)** and any answer choice less than **(C)**.

We have eliminated 54, **(C)**, and anything less than 54, **(A)** and **(B)**. Notice that we only have two answer choices left, so if **(D)** is not correct, we know **(E)** must be right. This is the strength of the back-solving method. If you start at **(C)** and can determine whether it's too small or too large, then you have to check at most one other answer choice to find the answer.

Let's go now to the next higher answer choice, **(D)**.

8. Employee X is paid $12.50 an hour no matter how many hours he works per week. Employee Y is paid $10 an hour for the first 30 hours she works in a week and is paid 1.5 times that for every hour over that. On a certain week, both employees worked the same number of hours and were paid the same amount. How many hours did each employee work that week?

- ⬭ ~~48~~
- ⬭ ~~50~~
- ⬭ ~~54~~
- ⬭ 60
- ⬭ 64

In 60 hours, employee X will earn 60 × $12.50 = $750.

In 60 hours, employee Y will earn 30 × $10 + 30 × $15 = 300 + 450 = $750.

Both employees earn the same amount, so **(D)** is correct.

CONCLUSION

If you practice picking numbers and back-solving, you will improve your Problem Solving performance. While these two strategies may not prove useful on all problems, they are great for simplifying complex word problems, which are often the hardest questions on the Quantitative section.

PROBLEM SOLVING PRACTICE SET

Directions: Solve the problem and choose the best answer.

Notes:

1. Unless otherwise indicated, the figures accompanying these questions have been drawn as accurately as possible and may be used as sources of information for answering the questions.

2. All figures lie in a plane except where noted.

3. All numbers used are real numbers.

1. If n is an even number, which of the following must be odd?

   ○ $\dfrac{3n}{2}$ $\dfrac{3(2)}{2} = 3$ $\dfrac{3(4)}{2} = 6$

   ○ $2(n-1)$ $2(2-1) = 2$

   ○ $n(n+1)$ $2(2+1) = 6$

   ○ $\dfrac{n}{2} + 1$ $\dfrac{2}{2} + 1 = 2$

   ☑ $2n + 1$ $2(2) + 1 = 5$

2. The cost to rent a boat for a fishing trip is x dollars, which is to be shared equally among the people taking the trip. If 12 people go on the trip rather than 20, how many more dollars, in terms of x, will it cost per person? $x = 60$

   ○ $\dfrac{x}{8}$ $= 60$ $12 \div 60 = 5$

   ○ $\dfrac{x}{12}$ $= 60$ $20 \div 60 = 3$

   ○ $\dfrac{x}{16}$ $= 60$

   ○ $\dfrac{x}{20}$ $= 60$ ③ 2 more per person

   ✗ $\dfrac{x}{30}$ $= 60$ ②

3. In a certain school, the ratio of boys to girls is 3 to 7. If there are 84 more girls than boys, how many boys are there?

○ 36

○ 48 ~boys

○ 63 $+84 = 147$ girls

$\frac{63}{3} \cdot \frac{147}{7}$

$21 \vdots 21$

○ 84

○ 147

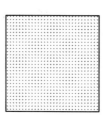

4. The diagram shown represents a square garden. If each side of the garden is increased in length by 50 percent, by what percent is the area of the garden increased?

○ 50%

○ 100%

⊗ 125%

○ 150%

○ 225%

$10 \quad \boxed{}^{10} = 100 \text{ sq ft}$

↑ by 50%

$15 \quad \boxed{}^{15} = 225 \text{ sq ft}$

$225 - 100 = 125 \text{ sq ft.}$

5. A water tower is filled to $\frac{3}{4}$ of its capacity. If $\frac{3}{5}$ of the water it is currently

    holding were to be released, what fraction of its capacity would it hold?

    ○ $\frac{3}{20}$

    ○ $\frac{1}{4}$

    ⊘ $\frac{3}{10}$

    ○ $\frac{2}{5}$

    ○ $\frac{9}{20}$

6. The "interlock" of two sets is defined as the average (arithmetic mean) of the
    elements that are common to both sets. If set M contains 12 consecutive integers,
    the greatest of which is 18, and set N contains 17 consecutive integers, the
    greatest of which is 30, what is the value of the interlock of sets M and N?

    ○ 14.5

    ⊗ 16

    ○ 22

    ○ 24

    ○ 32

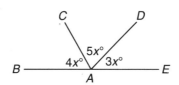

7. $\dfrac{a+b+c}{x+y+z}$ = $\dfrac{180}{(360-a)+(360-b)+(360-c)}$

$(360)3 - (+c + b + a)$

$(360)3 - 180$

$1080 \quad 900 \quad 180$

○ $\dfrac{1}{6}$

✗ $\dfrac{1}{5}$

○ $\dfrac{1}{4}$ $\dfrac{180}{900} = \dfrac{1}{5}$

○ $\dfrac{1}{3}$

> $c° = 360° - z$

> $b° = 360° - y$

> $a° = 360° - x$

$a + x = b + y = c + z = 360°$

$a + b + c = 180°$

$x = 360 - a$

$y = 360 - b$

$z = 360 - c$

○ It cannot be determined from the information given.

8. What is the degree measure of angle *CAE* shown?

○ 15

○ 45

○ 75

✗ 120

○ 135

$4x + 5x + 3x = 180°$

$12x = 180°$

$x = 15$

$\angle CAE = 5x + 3x$

$5(15) + 3(15)$

$75 + 45$

120

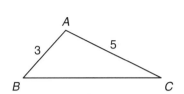

BC must be shorter than 8

9. In the figure shown, which of the following could be the length of *BC* ?

    ○ 1
    ○ 2
    ⊗ 5
    ○ 8
    ○ 9

10. Machine A can produce $\frac{1}{8}$ of a ton of nails in one hour. Machine B can produce $\frac{1}{12}$ of a ton of nails in one hour. Working together at their individual rates, how long would it take the two machines to produce one ton of nails?

    ○ 4 hours
    ⊗ 4 hours 48 minutes
    ○ 5 hours
    ○ 6 hours 20 minutes
    ○ 10 hours

$5 \times \frac{1}{8} = \frac{5}{8}$

$5 \times \frac{1}{12} = \frac{5}{12}$

$\frac{5}{8} + \frac{5}{12} = \frac{15}{24} + \frac{10}{24} = \frac{25}{24}$

$1\frac{1}{24}$

ANSWERS AND EXPLANATIONS

1. (E)

Try picking an even number for n to plug into the answer choices, such as 2. Discard all answer choices that do not give you an odd answer.

(A): $\dfrac{3n}{2} = \dfrac{3 \times 2}{2} = 3$. This is odd. Keep **(A)** for now.

(B): $2(n - 1) = 2(2 - 1) = 2$. This is not odd, so eliminate it.

(C): $n(n + 1) = 2(2 + 1) = 6$. This is not odd, so eliminate it.

(D): $\dfrac{n}{2} + 1 = \dfrac{2}{2} + 1 = 2$. This is not odd, so eliminate it.

(E): $2n + 1 = 2(2) + 1 = 5$. This is odd, so keep it for now.

Now try picking a different even number for n, such as 4.

(A): $\dfrac{3n}{2} = \dfrac{3 \times 4}{2} = \dfrac{12}{2} = 6$. This is not odd, so you can eliminate it.

The answer must be **(E)**. Let's check it.

(E): $2n + 1 = 2(4) + 1 = 9$. This is odd. Bingo!

2. (E)

Pick a number for x, making sure that the number you pick works well with the numbers in the problem. Because the numbers involved in the question stem are 12 and 20, you want a number that both 12 and 20 divide into evenly, so try $x = 60$. If 12 people go on the trip, the cost will be $5 per person. If 20 people go on the trip, the cost will be $3 per person. Consequently, the additional cost per person will be $2, and 2 is the target number.

(A): $\dfrac{x}{8} = 60 \div 8$, which is not 2, so you can eliminate this.

(B): $\dfrac{x}{12} = 60 \div 12 = 5$, which is not 2, so you can eliminate it.

(C): $\dfrac{x}{16} = 60 \div 16$, which is not 2, so you can eliminate it.

(D): $\dfrac{x}{20} = 60 \div 20 = 3$, which is not 2, so you can eliminate it.

(E): $\dfrac{x}{30} = 60 \div 30 = 2$. This is it!

3. (C)

Use back-solving on this one. The correct answer will yield a ratio of boys to girls of 3 to 7, when there are 84 more girls than boys. Start with **(C)**.

(C): If there are 63 boys, there are 63 + 84 = 147 girls, so the ratio of boys to girls is 63 ÷ 147 = 9 ÷ 21 = 3 ÷ 7. This is the same as a ratio of 3:7, which is just what you want. Because you found the answer straight away, there is no need to check any of the other answer choices.

4. (C)

Like almost all percent problems where no actual values are given, this is a great question to try picking numbers on. Because you are dealing with a square garden, both sides are the same, and the area is side × side. Make the original dimensions 10 ft. × 10 ft. for an original area of 100 sq. ft. Thus, if we increase each side length by 50 percent, the new dimensions would be 15 ft. × 15 ft. for a new area of 225 sq. ft. Consequently, the amount of increase is (225 − 100) = 125 sq. ft., which of course is 125 percent of 100 sq. ft.—which is why we love to use 100 in percent problems. **(C)** is correct.

5. (C)

Here you want to pick a number for the capacity of the water tower, making sure the number works well with the fractions in the problem. What number works well with $\dfrac{3}{4}$ and $\dfrac{3}{5}$? How about 20 gallons? Thus, if the tower is filled to $\dfrac{3}{4}$ of its capacity, it contains 15 gallons, and if $\dfrac{3}{5}$ of that were to be released, 9 gallons would be released, leaving 6 gallons. Because there are 6 of the original 20 gallons left, the tower would be left holding $\dfrac{6}{20} = \dfrac{3}{10}$ of its capacity.

6. (B)

In this problem, you're given an unfamiliar word, *interlock*. Don't panic when you see an unfamiliar term like this. The test will always define it for you. Make sure that you understand the definition; it's the key to this sort of problem. Read carefully to determine exactly what the term means. Basically the *interlock* is defined as the average of the numbers that are common to two sets. Run the numbers you are given into the definition. Set M contains the integers 7, 8, 9, 10, 11, 12, 13, 14, 15, 16, 17, and 18. Set N contains the integers 14, 15, 16, 17, 18 ... 30. The numbers common to both sets are 14, 15, 16, 17, and 18. Because these numbers are consecutive, and there is an odd number of these integers, the average is just the middle number: 16.

7. (B)

Remember that there are 360° around any point and that the interior angles of a triangle add up to 180°. From the first fact, you get that $a + x = b + y = c + z = 360$. From the second fact you get that $a + b = c = 180$. Therefore, $x = 360 - a$, $y = 360 - b$, and $z = 360 - c$. Plug these into the ratio given:

$$\frac{a+b+c}{x+y+z} = \frac{a+b+c}{360-a+360-b+360-c}$$

$$= \frac{a+b+c}{360+360+360-a-b-c}$$

$$= \frac{a+b+c}{360+360+360-(a-b-c)}$$

$$= \frac{180}{360+360+360-180}$$

$$= \frac{180}{900}$$

$$= \frac{1}{5}$$

8. (D)

Remember that a straight line has 180 degrees. That means that if you add the measures of angles *BAC*, *CAD*, and *DAE*, you'll get 180. Therefore, $4x + 5x + 3x = 180$, or $12x = 180$. Dividing by 12 on both sides yields $x = 15$. Be careful, however;

that's not your answer. You need to find the measure of angle *CAE*, which is the sum of the measures of angles *CAD* and *DAE*. That's 5(15) + 3(15), or 8(15) = 120.

9. (C)

In a triangle, each side must be shorter than the other two sides combined; otherwise, the sides couldn't meet at the three vertices. For instance, if *BC* were 1, *BA* and *BC* together would only be 4, meaning that they could not stretch from point *A* to point *C*. If *BC* were 2, *BA* and *BC* together would only be 5, meaning that they could only stretch from point *A* to point *C* if they were collinear—that is, a straight line segment exactly like *AC*. However, then *ABC* wouldn't be a triangle. By the same token, *BC* can't be 8 or 9, because *AB* and *AC* together measure only 8. The only possible value for *BC* here is 5. When *BC* = 5, the sum of the lengths of any two sides is greater than the length of the remaining side.

10. (B)

Start with **(C)**. Remember, you want a combined production of 1 ton. If the machines work for 5 hours, then machine A makes $5 \times \frac{1}{8} = \frac{5}{8}$ tons of nails, and machine B makes $5 \times \frac{1}{12} = \frac{5}{12}$ tons of nails. Then the total is $\frac{5}{8} + \frac{5}{12} = \frac{15}{24} + \frac{10}{24} = \frac{25}{24} = 1\frac{1}{24}$. This is greater than 1, so **(C)** and any choice greater than **(C)** can be eliminated. Now try a smaller number.

Because **(B)** is hard to work with, go to **(A)**. If the machines work for 4 hours, then machine A makes $4 \times \frac{1}{8} = \frac{4}{8}$ tons of nails. Machine B makes $4 \times \frac{1}{12} = \frac{4}{12}$ tons of nails. The total is then $\frac{4}{8} + \frac{4}{12} = \frac{12}{24} + \frac{8}{24} = \frac{20}{24}$. This is too small.

Because **(A)** is too small and **(C)** is too large, the correct answer must lie between the two. That is, the correct answer is **(B)**.

CHAPTER 8: QUANTITATIVE COMPARISONS

INTRODUCTION TO QUANTITATIVE COMPARISONS

This lesson will introduce you to the most important math question type—Quantitative Comparisons, or QCs. A full half of the math questions on the test are QCs, so knowing how to handle them is essential to a good math score.

Although they might look confusing at first, QCs should actually take you less time to answer than regular math problems. This is because QCs simply ask you to compare two quantities to determine which, if either, is greater. You don't need to do a lot of calculation to find a numerical answer.

We will explore the variety of ways to attack QCs questions later, but first you need to familiarize yourself with this question type. Let's start by looking at a typical Quantitative Comparison.

ANATOMY OF A QUANTITATIVE COMPARISON QUESTION

Below is a typical Quantitative Comparison question, along with its directions.

Numbers: All numbers are real numbers.

Figures:

1. The location of points and angles is assumed to be in the order illustrated.

2. All the lines drawn as straight can be assumed to be straight.

3. All figures lie in the plane unless otherwise stated.

4. You cannot assume figures are drawn to scale unless otherwise stated.

Common information: Information concerning one or both of the quantities to be compared is centered above the two columns.

Directions: Compare the quantities in Column A and Column B, then choose the answer choice that defines the relationship between the columns.

1.

$$a > 7 > b > 0$$

Column A

$$\frac{a-7}{a}$$

Column B

$$\frac{7-a}{b}$$

- ◯ Column A is greater than Column B.
- ◯ Column B is greater than Column B.
- ◯ Both columns are equal.
- ◯ The relationship between the columns cannot be determined.

NUMBERS NOTE

"All numbers are real numbers," means you are not dealing with imaginary numbers such as i; that is, $\sqrt{1}$.

FIGURES NOTES

1. The location of points and angles is assumed to be in the order illustrated.

This means that the diagrams are accurate insofar as the order of points. In other words, you can assume in the following diagram that *ABC* is a triangle and that the points correspond to the angles as marked.

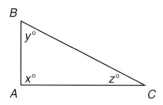

However, you cannot assume that lengths and angles are accurate; that is, that side AC is longer than side AB or that x is 90 degrees. It's important to note that QC geometry diagrams are often deliberately misleading. If there is a diagram, ask yourself whether or not it is drawn to scale.

2. All the lines drawn as straight can be assumed to be straight.

This means that lines that look straight are. (They may appear very slightly jagged due to the limited resolution of the computer screen.)

3. All figures lie in the plane unless otherwise stated.

This means that they will tell you if you are working with a three-dimensional figure such as a cube, sphere, or cylinder.

4. You cannot assume figures are drawn to scale unless otherwise stated.

Lengths and angles may not be accurately represented. For example, unless you were told, you could not assume the following diagram on the GRE was a square:

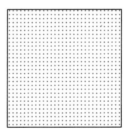

The lengths need not be all the same or the angles right angles. It could just as easily look like this:

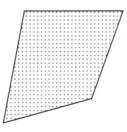

All you know is that the shape has four sides and that those sides are straight.

CENTERED (COMMON) INFORMATION

There is often information centered between the columns. You will need this information to answer the question, so pay close attention to what it tells you.

DIRECTIONS

The directions ask you to *compare the quantities* in the columns, *not to calculate them.* There are four possible relationships between the columns—one or the other is larger, they are equal, or you can't tell.

COLUMNS

You are asked to compare the columns, so don't waste time actually finding numeric values.

In this case, the common information tells you that a, $a - 7$, and b are all positive and that $7 - a$ must be negative. Therefore, column A must be positive, and it is greater than column B, which must be negative. Even if you can't find actual values for column A and column B, you have enough information to compare them.

ANSWER CHOICES

The four answer choices are always the same and always in the same order. They are as follows:

Choice 1: Pick choice 1 when you know that the quantity in column A is definitely greater than the quantity in column B.

Choice 2: Pick choice 2 when you know that the quantity in column B is definitely greater than the quantity in column A.

Choice 3: Pick choice 3 when you know that the two quantities must always be equal.

Choice 4: Pick choice 4 when there is insufficient information to determine which column is greater. If in some cases one column is greater and in other cases it's not, pick choice 4. Choice 4 will only be the answer when there is an unknown value, or variable, in one of the columns.

QUANTITATIVE COMPARISONS STRATEGIES

Compare, don't calculate!

QCs are designed to be done quickly. Remember, you don't need to find a numerical answer; you just need to compare the two quantities.

However, this is often quite difficult to do, because the test maker puts the items in each column in different forms.

Which of the following is the easier question to answer?

Which is greater: $3\sqrt{2}$ or $2\sqrt{3}$?

Which is greater: 18 or 12?

Now obviously, the second question is extremely easy to answer, which is why you will never see a QC where you simply have to compare 18 to 12.

However, the first question is asking almost the same thing. Square both numbers to get rid of the radical signs, and you'll find you are comparing 18 to 12, so $3\sqrt{2}$ must be larger than $2\sqrt{3}$.

This is the key skill on QCs—finding the easiest way to get the columns into forms that can be compared. Fortunately, there are several strategies that can help you do this. The simplest of these strategies is changing one column to look more like the other.

MAKING THE COLUMNS ALIKE

Use this strategy when the columns contain different kinds of numbers that can be expressed in the same way.

The test makers often make things slightly more difficult by altering the way that one of the columns is expressed. For instance, percents, ratios, decimals, and fractions are all really the same thing, a way of comparing by division. Instead of asking you simply to compare two fractions, however, the test maker might ask you to compare a percent to a fraction. If you have a mixture of these sorts of quantities in each column, turn them all into similar terms so they can be compared easily.

Try this in the following question. Turn 30 percent into a fraction and 0.5 into a fraction and see how much simpler the comparison becomes.

2.

Column A	Column B
30 percent of 0.5	$\dfrac{1}{5} \times \dfrac{1}{2}$

(handwritten annotations: $\dfrac{3}{10}$ above "30 percent of", $\dfrac{1}{2}$ above "0.5")

◯ Column A is greater than column B.

◯ Column B is greater than column A.

◯ Both columns are equal.

◯ The relationship between the columns cannot be determined.

30 percent as a fraction = $\dfrac{3}{10}$.

0.5 as a fraction = $\dfrac{1}{2}$.

We now have $\dfrac{3}{10} \times \dfrac{1}{2}$ in column A and $\dfrac{1}{5} \times \dfrac{1}{2}$ in column B. We know that $\dfrac{3}{10}$ is greater than $\dfrac{1}{5}$ because $\dfrac{1}{5} = \dfrac{2}{10}$. Therefore, $\dfrac{3}{10} \times \dfrac{1}{2}$ is greater than $\dfrac{1}{5} \times \dfrac{1}{2}$. Notice that we don't have to bother to do the multiplication, because both sides are being multiplied by one-half. It's enough to know that $\dfrac{3}{10}$ is greater than $\dfrac{1}{5}$.

(A): Column A is greater than column B.

Any question that mixes fractions, percents, ratios, and rates can nearly always be solved using this technique. Here's a slightly harder example.

3. Bill has only nickels, dimes, and quarters. The ratio of nickels to dimes in Bill's pocket is 2:3, while the ratio of dimes to quarters is 1: 4.

Column A	Column B
Ratio of nickels to quarters in Bill's pocket	$\dfrac{1}{2}$

◯ Column A is greater than column B.

◯ Column B is greater than column A.

◯ Both columns are equal.

◯ The relationship between the columns cannot be determined.

The ratio of nickels to dimes as a fraction is $= \dfrac{N}{D} = \dfrac{2}{3}$.

The ratio of dimes to quarters as a fraction is $= \dfrac{D}{Q} = \dfrac{1}{4}$.

Therefore, the ratio of nickels to quarters is $\dfrac{N}{D} \times \dfrac{D}{Q} = \dfrac{N}{Q}$. That is, $\dfrac{2}{3} \times \dfrac{1}{4} = \dfrac{2}{12}$.

Column A contains $\dfrac{2}{12}$, which is a lot less than the $\dfrac{1}{2}$ in column B.

(B): Column B is greater than column A.

Another thing to watch for is units. Make sure the units in separate columns are the same.

4.   **Column A**   **Column B**
        The number of minutes in   The number of minutes
            2 hours 20 minutes   in 2.20 hours

- ◯ Column A is greater than column B.
- ◯ Column B is greater than column A.
- ◯ Both columns are equal.
- ◯ The relationship between the columns cannot be determined.

Whatever you do, don't assume that two columns that look the same are the same. If the columns look equal, as in this case with a 2 and a 20 in each column, they almost never will be. This is a very common trap on GRE QCs.

The quantities in the columns need to be changed so that they are in the same form. Column A is in hours and minutes; column B is in hours and tenths of an hour. It will probably be easiest to change column B.

You know that 0.20 hours is $\dfrac{2}{10}$ of an hour, which is $\dfrac{2}{10} \times 60$ minutes $= 12$ minutes.

Now you have 2 hours 20 minutes in column A and 2 hours 12 minutes in column B.

(A): Column A is greater than column B.

COMPARING PIECE BY PIECE

Use this technique when each column contains a series of separate items.

Sometimes, each of the columns contains several values being added, subtracted, or multiplied together. These problems would seem to involve a painful amount of calculating, but usually you can compare the separate pieces in each column. Try comparing the following quantities.

5.

Column A	Column B
$\dfrac{1}{2} + \dfrac{4}{5} + \dfrac{7}{10} + \dfrac{9}{7}$	$\dfrac{1}{3} + \dfrac{4}{7} + \dfrac{8}{9} + \dfrac{6}{11}$

⊘ Column A is greater than column B.

◯ Column B is greater than column A.

◯ Both columns are equal.

◯ The relationship between the columns cannot be determined.

Let's look at column A: $\dfrac{1}{2} + \dfrac{4}{5} + \dfrac{7}{10} + \dfrac{9}{7}$ is a tedious calculation.

Let's look at column B: $\dfrac{1}{3} + \dfrac{4}{7} + \dfrac{8}{9} + \dfrac{6}{11}$ is another tedious calculation.

You won't have to add up any of these expressions if you just compare the fractions one at a time.

Remember, you don't have to compare them in order. What you are trying to determine is whether every fraction in one column is larger than a corresponding fraction in the other, like so.

Look at the first fraction in each column: $\dfrac{1}{2} > \dfrac{1}{3}$.

Compare the next fractions: $\dfrac{4}{5} > \dfrac{4}{7}$. So far column A is greater.

Compare these two fractions: $\dfrac{7}{10} > \dfrac{6}{11}$.

Compare the remaining two fractions: $\dfrac{9}{7} > \dfrac{8}{9}$.

For every piece of column B, there is a corresponding larger piece of column A. Therefore, column A must be larger.

(A): Column A is greater than column B.

The following exercise helps you practice comparing piece by piece. Remember, every bit of one column must be greater than each corresponding piece of the other column for this shortcut to be effective. That is, you want to find pairs of numbers, and in each pair, the same column must always contain the bigger number for you to determine the relationship in this fashion.

Directions: Match each part of column A with a part of column B that is less than that part. Write your answers in the space provided.

Column A	Correct Answer	Column B
$\sqrt{37} + 10$		$6 + \sqrt{99}$
$\dfrac{1}{9} + \dfrac{1}{7} - \dfrac{1}{4}$		$\dfrac{1}{8} + \dfrac{1}{10} - \dfrac{1}{3}$
$y + w$		$z + x$

You should have come up with the following piece-by-piece comparisons.

Column A	Correct Answer	Column B
$\sqrt{37} + 10$	$\sqrt{37} > 6$ $10 > \sqrt{99}$	$6 + \sqrt{99}$
$\dfrac{1}{9} + \dfrac{1}{7} - \dfrac{1}{4}$	$\dfrac{1}{9} > \dfrac{1}{10}$ $\dfrac{1}{7} > \dfrac{1}{8}$ $-\dfrac{1}{4} > -\dfrac{1}{3}$	$\dfrac{1}{8} + \dfrac{1}{10} - \dfrac{1}{3}$
$y + w$	$w > x$ $y > z$	$z + x$

You don't always have to find that all of the pairs contain one larger and one smaller element. If any of the pairs contain elements of the same size, then that pair can be ignored.

6.

Column A	Column B
$8^2 + 7^2 + 6^2$	$36 + 50 + 65$

○ Column A is greater than column B.

⊗ Column B is greater than column A.

○ Both columns are equal.

○ The relationship between the columns cannot be determined.

Start by squaring each of the numbers in column A:

$8^2 = 64 < 65$
$7^2 = 49 < 50$
$6^2 = 36$

Each part of column B (36, 50, 65) is greater than or equal to a corresponding part of column A (36, 49, 64), so column B is larger.

(B): Column B is greater than column A.

DOING THE SAME THING TO BOTH COLUMNS

You can change the values in both columns as long as you do the same thing to both columns and don't multiply or divide by a negative number.

Some QC questions become a lot clearer when you change the appearance of the values in both columns

There are several things that you can do that do not change the relationship between the columns. You can always safely

- add or subtract the same value from both columns.
- multiply or divide both columns by the same *positive* value without altering the relationship. Be careful though. Multiplying or dividing by a quantity that is (or could be) negative does not work.

• square both columns. (Just make sure that neither side is negative before you do so.)

Try this strategy on the following problem to get something that is easy to compare in each column. Try simplifying the columns by doing the same thing to each one step at a time.

7. $z > 1$

Column A   Column B

$$\frac{z}{z-1} - 1$$ $$\frac{1}{z-1} - 1$$

○ Column A is greater than column B.

○ Column B is greater than column A.

○ Both columns are equal.

○ The relationship between the columns cannot be determined.

Simplify the columns one step at a time.

First, get rid of the 1 by adding 1 to both columns:

Column A   Column B

$$\frac{z}{z-1} - 1 + 1 = \frac{z}{z-1}$$ $$\frac{1}{z-1} - 1 + 1 = \frac{1}{z-1}$$

Now, simplify the remaining fractions by multiplying both columns by $z - 1$.

Column A   Column B

$$\frac{z}{z-1} \times (z-1) = z$$ $$\frac{1}{z-1} \times (z-1) = 1$$

Because the centered information tells you that $z > 1$, the correct answer is **(A)**, column A is greater than column B.

The columns were difficult to compare at first, but by doing the same thing, step by step, they were greatly simplified. Notice that we knew we could multiply both columns by $z - 1$ because z is greater than 1, so $z - 1$ has to be greater than 0. Never multiply both columns by any quantity that could be negative.

As long as you know you're not dealing with negative numbers, you can always square both columns. This is often the easiest way to get rid of annoying square roots.

8.

Column A	Column B
$\dfrac{\sqrt{5}}{\sqrt{3}}$	$\dfrac{5}{3}$

Column A	Column B
$\left(\dfrac{\sqrt{5}}{\sqrt{3}}\right)^2 = \dfrac{\left(\sqrt{5}\right)^2}{\left(\sqrt{3}\right)^2} = \dfrac{5}{3}$ $= 1\frac{2}{3}$	$\left(\dfrac{5}{3}\right)^2 = \dfrac{5^2}{3^2} = \dfrac{25}{9}$ $= 2\frac{7}{9}$

Column A is a bit greater than 1, while column B is greater than 2. Therefore, column B is bigger.

(B): Column is greater than column A.

PICKING NUMBERS

If the QC has variables, you can almost always solve the question by picking numbers.

Picking numbers makes abstract problems more concrete and manageable. It also can be used to eliminate wrong answer choices quickly on QCs whose answer is **(D)**, the relationship between the columns cannot be determined.

- Write down "A B C D" on your scratch paper and eliminate as you go along. After trying out your first number, you will always be able to eliminate two answer choices. The correct answer will either be the relationship you find with your first set of numbers or **(D)**, the relationship between the columns cannot be determined.

- Try to make the relationship between the columns change between picks. Try to get a different result with your second set of numbers by picking different types of numbers.

- Think about picking negative numbers, fractions, zero, and one, because these numbers often produce different results than positive integers.

9. $x = yz$ $z > 0$

Column A	Column B
x	y

○ Column A is greater than column B.

○ Column B is greater than column A.

○ Both columns are equal.

○ The relationship between the columns cannot be determined.

You are given three variables in this QC, so it is an excellent time to pick numbers. Remember when picking numbers on QCs, you must pick numbers that conform to the centered information. Therefore, $x = yz$ and $z > 0$. Because z must be greater than zero, let's pick $z = 1$. If $z = 1$, any values you pick for x and y must be equal. Because you picked numbers and found that the columns can be equal, you know the correct answer is either **(C)** or **(D)**. Now try to pick values that give you a different relationship. If $z = 2$ and $y = 1$, x must equal 2. In this case column A is greater. The relationship changes, so **(D)** is correct. Remember, when picking numbers on QCs, once you find two different relationships, stop picking numbers and choose **(D)**.

When picking numbers, remember also that you are trying to pick numbers that establish two different relationships. Pick numbers across categories in the following exercise to determine whether **(D)** is the correct answer.

PICKING NUMBERS EXERCISE

Directions: Pick numbers and write your answers in the space provided. When you get two different relationships between the columns, the answer must be **(D)**. Try to establish whether the answer is **(D)** in as few picks as possible.

$$X > 0$$

Column A	Correct Answer	Column B
X^2		X^3

$$X \neq 1, X \neq 0, X \neq -1$$

Column A	Correct Answer	Column B
X^2		X^4

Column A	Correct Answer	Column B
$(X + 1)(X)(X - 1)$		$(X + 2)^2$

Column A	Correct Answer	Column B
$(X + 1)^2$		X^3

Solution:

$$X > 0$$

Column A	Correct Answer	Column B
X^2	(D)	X^3
$X = 1 \Rightarrow 1; X = 2 \Rightarrow 4$		$X = 1 \Rightarrow 1; X = 2 \Rightarrow 8$

$$X \neq 1, X \neq 0, X \neq -1$$

Column A	Correct Answer	Column B
X^2	(D)	X^4
$X = 0.5 \Rightarrow 0.25; X = 2 \Rightarrow 4$		$X = 0.5 \Rightarrow 0.0625; X = 2 \Rightarrow 16$

Column A	Correct Answer	Column B
$(X + 1)(X)(X - 1)$	(B)	$(X + 2)^2$
$X = 1 \Rightarrow \emptyset; X = -2 \Rightarrow -6$		$X = 1 \Rightarrow 9; X = -2 \Rightarrow \emptyset$

Column A	Correct Answer	Column B
$(X + 1)^2$	(A)	X^3
$X = 1 \Rightarrow 4; X = -1 \Rightarrow \emptyset$		$X = 1 \Rightarrow 1; X = -1 \Rightarrow -1$

Let's look at another QC that involves picking numbers.

10. $z < 1$

Column A	Column B
$z - 1$	$1 - z$

○ Column A is greater than column B.

○ Column B is greater than column A.

○ Both columns are equal.

○ The relationship between the columns cannot be determined.

Pick numbers that conform to the centered information, $z < 1$. You can pick positive fractions, zero, and negative numbers for z. If $z = 0$, then column A $= 0 - 1 = -1$, and column B $= 1 - 0 = 1$. Therefore, column B is greater, and the correct answer is either **(B)** or **(D)**.

Now try a fraction like 0.5. If $z = 0.5$, then column A $= 0.5 - 1 = -0.5$, and column B $= 1 - 0.5 = 0.5$. Column B is still greater.

Note the trend and try a negative value for z. If $z = -2$, then column A $= -2 - 1 = -3$, and column B $= 1 - -2 = 1 + 2 = 3$. Column B is still greater.

(B): Column B is greater than column A.

CONCLUSION

If you practice manipulating the columns so that they allow for easy comparison and if you avoid time-consuming and unnecessary calculations, you will vastly improve your performance on QCs. Remember that the test maker builds in quick ways to compare the columns, so developing an eye for spotting these shortcuts will pay off with a higher GRE Quantitative score. In time, you will find that QCs are the Quantitative questions you can handle in the shortest amount of time.

QUANTITATIVE COMPARISONS PRACTICE SET

Numbers: All numbers are real numbers.

Figures:

1. The location of points and angles is assumed to be in the order illustrated.

2. All the lines drawn as straight can be assumed to be straight.

3. All figures lie in the plane unless otherwise stated.

4. You cannot assume figures are drawn to scale unless otherwise stated.

Common information: Information concerning one or both of the quantities to be compared is centered above the two columns.

Directions: Compare the quantities in Column A and Column B, then choose the answer choice that defines the relationship between the columns.

1.

Column A	Column B
29 percent of 38	$\dfrac{29 \times 30}{100}$

- ⊗ Column A is greater than column B.
- ◯ Column B is greater than column A.
- ◯ Both columns are equal.
- ◯ The relationship between the columns cannot be determined.

2.

Column A	Column B
$x(x-1)^2$	$x^2 - x$

- ◯ Column A is greater than column B.
- ◯ Column B is greater than column A.
- ◯ Both columns are equal.
- ⊗ The relationship between the columns cannot be determined.

3. The diameter of circle O is the same as the length of a side of square S.

Column A	Column B
The area of square S	The area of circle O

- ⊗ Column A is greater than column B.
- ◯ Column B is greater than column A.
- ◯ Both columns are equal.
- ◯ The relationship between the columns cannot be determined.

4.

Column A	Column B
$(-9)^8$	$(-8)^9$

- ◯ Column A is greater than column B.
- ◯ Column B is greater than column A.
- ◯ Both columns are equal.
- ◯ The relationship between the columns cannot be determined.

5. AC is a diagonal of square $ABCD$.

Column A	Column B
The ratio of the length of diagonal AC to the perimeter of $ABCD$	1:2

- ◯ Column A is greater than column B.
- ◯ Column B is greater than column A.
- ◯ Both columns are equal.
- ◯ The relationship between the columns cannot be determined.

6.

$$3^5 = \frac{3^{15}}{3^x}$$

Column A	Column B
$x = 10$	3

⊗ Column A is greater than column B.

⊙ Column B is greater than column A.

⊙ Both columns are equal.

⊙ The relationship between the columns cannot be determined.

7. z is an integer. The remainder when z is divided by 5 is 2.

Column A	Column B
The remainder when $3z$ is divided by 5	2

⊙ Column A is greater than column B.

⊙ Column B is greater than column A.

⊙ Both columns are equal.

⊙ The relationship between the columns cannot be determined.

8.

Column A	Column B
$(2\sqrt{5}+1)(2\sqrt{5}-1)$	9

$(2\sqrt5)^2 - (1)^2$

⊗ Column A is greater than column B.

⊙ Column B is greater than column A.

⊙ Both columns are equal.

⊙ The relationship between the columns cannot be determined.

$4(5) - 1$

$20 - 1$

$\boxed{19}$

9.

Column A	Column B
The number of distinct	The number of distinct
prime factors of 45	prime factors of 75

○ Column A is greater than column B.

○ Column B is greater than column A.

⊗ Both columns are equal.

○ The relationship between the columns cannot be determined.

10.

Column A	Column B
$\left(\sqrt{5^3}\right)^2$	$\left(5\sqrt{5}\right)^2$

$5^3 = 5 \times 5 \times 5$
25×5

$25(5)$

○ Column A is greater than column B.

○ Column B is greater than column A.

⊗ Both columns are equal.

○ The relationship between the columns cannot be determined.

ANSWERS AND EXPLANATIONS

1. (C)

Make the columns look more alike by changing column A into a mathematical expression. Twenty-nine percent is the same thing as 29 hundredths; that is, $\frac{29}{100}$. Therefore, 29 percent of 38 is $\frac{29}{100} \times 38 = \frac{29 \times 30}{100}$. The columns are equal, **(C)**.

Note that there was no need to do any calculation. Merely getting the columns into the same form was enough.

2. (D)

Questions with variables are good candidates to try picking numbers on. First try something easy, such as 1. If $x = 1$, then column A becomes $x(x - 1)^2 = 1(1 - 1)^2 = 1(0)^2 = 0$. Column B becomes $x^2 - x = 1^2 - 1 = 0$. In this case, the columns are equal.

Now try another easy number, say $x = -1$. If $x = 0$, then column A becomes $x(x-1)^2$ $= -1(1-(-1))^2 = -1(2)^2 = -4$. Column B becomes $x^2 - x = (-1)^2 - (-1) = 1 + 1 = 2$. In this case, column B is greater.

Because more than one relationship is possible between the columns, the answer must be **(D)**.

3. **(A)**

In geometry questions, if you are not given a diagram, then you should quickly sketch one on your scratch paper. If you draw a square where one side is the diameter of a circle, you should get something like this.

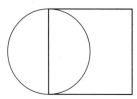

If you move the circle over, it fits within the square.

The square, and column A, is larger.

4. **(A)**

This is a classic QC question testing your knowledge of negative values and exponents. Any negative value raised to an even exponent is positive. Any negative value raised to an odd exponent is negative. So without calculating, you know that column A is positive and column B is negative. Therefore, **(A)** is correct.

5. (B)

A quick sketch of the figure is helpful.

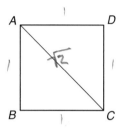

The diagonal is the hypotenuse of a 45-45-90 triangle, so if a side of the square has a length of 1, the length of the diagonal would be the square root of 2, which is about 1.4. The perimeter of a square is 4s, so a square with a side length of 1 has a perimeter of 4. Therefore, the ratio of the diagonal to the perimeter of the square is about 1.4:4. This is less than a 1:2 ratio, so **(B)** is correct.

6. (A)

When dividing values with the same base, you subtract the exponents. Learn what you can from the centered information: $3^5 = \dfrac{3^{15}}{3^x}$. Therefore, $5 = 15 - x$. Some quick algebra shows you that $x = 10$. Column A is greater; **(A)** is the correct answer.

7. (B)

Pick a value for z. If z leaves a remainder of 2 when divided by 5, z could be a number such as 7. Therefore, when $3z$ is divided by 5, the remainder would be the same as if 3(7), or 21, were divided by 5. The number 21 leaves a remainder of 1 when divided by 5. Therefore, column A has a value of 1. Column B is greater; **(B)** is the correct answer.

8. (A)

Notice that $(2\sqrt{5}+1)(2\sqrt{5}-1)$ is in a classic form. This simplifies to the difference between two squares. Therefore, the simplified expression is $(2\sqrt{5})^2 - (1)^2 = 4(5) - 1 = 20 - 1 = 19$. You know $19 > 9$, so column A is greater, and **(A)** is correct.

9. (C)

To find the number of distinct prime factors of a number, continue to break down factors of the number until you are left with only prime numbers. Remember that *distinct* simply means to count any repeated value only once. Therefore, 45 factors to 9×5, which further factors to $3 \times 3 \times 5$. The prime factors of 45 are 3, 3, and 5, and the distinct prime factors of 45 are 3 and 5. Likewise, 75 factors to 3×25, which further factors to $3 \times 5 \times 5$. The prime factors of 75 are 3, 5, and 5, and the distinct prime factors of 75 are 3 and 5. Each number has two distinct prime factors, so **(C)** is correct.

10. (C)

Simplify matters by squaring both sides. Begin with column A: $\sqrt{5^3}^2 = 5^3 = 125$.

Then square column B: $5\sqrt{5}^2 = 25(5) = 125$. Therefore, the columns are equal; **(C)** is the correct answer.

CHAPTER 9: DATA INTERPRETATION

INTRODUCTION TO DATA INTERPRETATION

Out of the 28 Quantitative questions on the test, about 4 or 5 will be Data Interpretation questions. Most likely, you will see two sets of graphs with two questions accompanying each.

Data Interpretation questions come in two parts, a visual representation of data in the form of graphs or charts and questions about this data.

Data Interpretation questions can seem difficult until you learn how to make the visual representation of the data work for you. We'll talk about this later, but first let's look at a typical Data Interpretation question.

ANATOMY OF A DATA INTERPRETATION QUESTION

Following is a typical Graph question, along with its directions.

> **Directions:** The questions in this set refer to the data provided. For each question, select the best answer from among those given.

Questions 1–2 are based on the following graph.

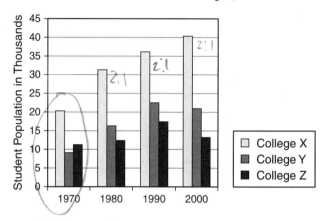

Note: Diagram drawn to scale

1. In which year was the ratio of the size of the student body at College X to the size of the student body at College Y the greatest?

   ◯ 1970

   ◯ 1980

   ◯ 1990

   ◯ 2000

   ◯ It cannot be determined from the information given.

DIRECTIONS

These are straightforward—use the data in the graphs to answer the question you are given.

INFORMATION

On the left of the screen, you will be told how many questions are in this graph set, and on the right, where you are in the section. Use this information to help you plan your time. If there are three questions in the graph set, invest a little extra time in examining the data before you answer the question.

TITLE

Read the title and get a sense of the topic of the graph. You must focus, especially when there are multiple graphs, on exactly what sort of information the graph is measuring.

LEGEND

This will tell you which colors or patterns are associated with which line or bar. Use this to make sure you are reading the right information off the graph.

GRAPH

This is where your data is displayed. Take a moment to examine the graph before you go to the question and look for any trends. Here, enrollments increase for each school each year, except for colleges Y and Z between 1990 and 2000. This is probably an important detail; you will almost certainly see a question based upon it.

UNITS

The units are the key to understanding graphs. Make sure you know what each axis measures and what units they are divided into.

On this question, there is one important point—the units in the vertical axis are the number of students *in thousands*.

NOTE

This simply means that the graph is drawn accurately.

QUESTION

Read this only after you have examined the graphs and worked out what they mean. Check carefully to make sure you know what you are dealing with. In this case you are only dealing with colleges X and Y, so ignore the darkest bars associated with college Z.

ANSWER CHOICES

The answer choices can give you clues to how to proceed. In many cases, if the answer choices are widely spaced, you can estimate values to make things easier.

DATA INTERPRETATION STRATEGIES

Save time by using the graphs to estimate and approximate values.

Graph questions can be great time wasters. First, GRE graphs are loaded with all sorts of unnecessary filler that is irrelevant to the question before you. Second, the numbers that you will be working with are often large and hard to manipulate. You don't get to use a calculator, so it is easy to make mistakes.

The first problem is easy to deal with: to get a handle on the information without wasting too much time on the graphs, you have to know what to look for and what to ignore. Take a few moments to examine the title and units and take note of the trends within the graph(s). If there's a scroll bar nearby, make sure to scroll down; there may be another graph hidden from view. Once you know a bit about what's contained in the graph(s), you'll know where to go to find the data you need to answer the question.

The second problem is trickier to handle. Graphs present information visually. People use them to make complex data easier to understand, so graph questions are full of shortcuts for test takers who are on their toes. Sometimes you'll want to do all the math. Many times, however, these problems are best solved by eyeballing and approximating.

> **Note:** The easiest and best approach to answering graph questions involves approximating and eliminating unlikely answer choices. You should get in the habit of approximating wherever you can on graph questions. You'll have a much easier time with these questions if you do.

EXAMINING THE GRAPHS

Graphs express information visually, making it easier to spot trends and make side-by-side comparisons.

It is often possible to answer a question simply by comparing the relative sizes and trends in a graph. We call the action of comparing without actually calculating values "eyeballing." It's often the quickest and easiest way to the answer because it requires a minimum of calculation.

Take a look at the following question. You could answer it by reading the values for student populations of colleges X and Y in each of the years from the graph and then calculating the ratio for each year. This is a lot of work and takes too long. It is far easier to answer this question by eyeballing.

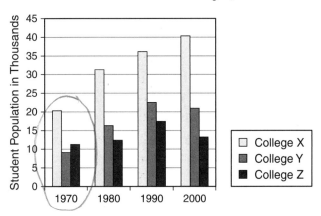

Student Bodies of Three State Colleges, 1970–2000

1. In which year was the ratio of the size of the student body at College X to the size of the student body at College Y the greatest?

    ○ 1970

    ○ 1980

    ○ 1990

    ○ 2000

    ○ It cannot be determined from the information given.

The year with the greatest ratio between college X and college Y will be the year when the lightly shaded bar (college X) is longest relative to the gray bar (college Y). You should be able to tell, just by eyeballing it, that 1970 is the only year shown in which the ratio is more than 2 to 1. The correct answer is **(A)**.

ESTIMATING AND APPROXIMATING

It is not always possible, however, to answer the question merely by examining the graphs. You will have to do some calculating.

These calculations become much easier, however, if you don't work with the exact values given but rather approximate these values. For instance, if you were asked to find the ratio of the number of students in college X to the number of students in college Y in 1970, chances are you wouldn't need to work out the actual ratio of 20.31:8.95. What is helpful is to note that the ratio is greater than 20:10 or 2:1.

How rough this approximation can be depends on how far apart the answer choices are in value. The further apart the answer choices, the more rough your estimations can be.

Take a look at the following question. It seems to require quite a bit of calculation involving the percent increase formula. You can make these calculations easier, however, by eliminating unlikely answers and estimating the values for the remaining choices.

Use this graph for the following question.

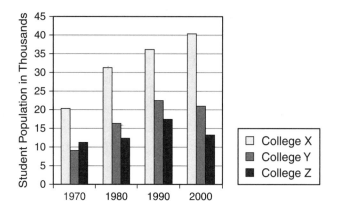

2. Which of the following student populations experienced the greatest percent increase over the years shown?

   ⊘ College X between 1970 and 1980

   ◯ College X between 1990 and 2000

   ◯ College Y between 1970 and 1980

   ◯ College Y between 1980 and 1990

   ◯ College Z between 1990 and 2000

Run through the years given, roughly calculating the percent increase. The percent increase formula is: $\dfrac{\text{Amount of increase}}{\text{Original (the smaller) amount}} \times 100\%$.

College X between 1970 and 1980: The population goes from about 20 to 30, a percent increase of 10/20 = 50 percent.

College X between 1990 and 2000: College X goes from about 36 to 40. This is nowhere near the 50 percent increase in **(A)**, so discard this answer choice without calculating.

College Y between 1970 and 1980: College Y goes from about 9 to 16, a percent increase of 7/9 = 78 percent.

College Y between 1980 and 1990: The population goes from about 17 to 22. Because it increased by less than a half, it must be less than the percent increase in **(A)**.

College Z between 1990 and 2000: The population actually falls between these years, so there is a percent decrease here.

(A) shows the greatest growth, so it is correct.

Notice how we were able to get the answer by only calculating two percents—and those pretty roughly.

MULTIPLE GRAPHS

Quite often you will have to deal with several graphs at once.

The most difficult feature of questions with multiple graphs is determining where to look to find the information you need. Always double-check the units and the scale, because they're likely to change from graph to graph.

> **Note:** Whenever you're given a graph question accompanied by a scroll bar, make sure to scroll down and see how many graphs accompany your question. Very often, not all the graphs will be visible!

Take a look at the following graph set, which details the scintillating subject of potato production in Canada. Three questions accompany this graph set. Notice how they differ quite radically in difficulty. The computer chooses the graph set based on the average difficulty of the questions in that set. Consequently, you are likely to get questions that are considerably harder or easier than your current scoring level.

Potato Production in Canada, 1998

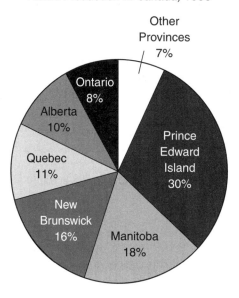

Total production = 1,359,040 metric tons

Province	Area Under Cultivation (in hectares)	Value of Crop (in millions of dollars)
Prince Edward Island	45,000	189
Manitoba	30,000	126
New Brunswick	23,000	86
Quebec	19,000	74
Alberta	13,000	67
Ontario	17,000	63
Other Provinces	9,000	32

3. In 1998, approximately how many metric tons of potatoes were grown in Manitoba?

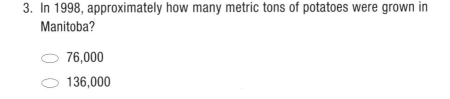

    76,000

    136,000

    180,000

    245,000

    342,000

This is an easy graph question (the first one often is).

First, figure out which graph you're dealing with. In this case, it's the pie chart. You need to find the total yield in metric tonnage of potatoes in Manitoba. The percent yield for Manitoba is 18 percent, which is a little less than 20 percent, or a fifth, of Canada's total potato yield. The approximate value of the total metric tonnage for Canada is about 1,360,000 metric tons. Dividing this by 5 will give you 272,000 metric tons, which is a little more than the yield for Manitoba. The only answer choice that is close is 245,000 metric tons is **(D)**.

Because this is the first question in a set of multiple graph questions, you should have taken a few seconds familiarizing yourself with the graphs before you plunged into the question. Fortunately, as is the case here, the first question tends to be a softball. As long as you know how to read a pie chart and convert the percents given into actual amounts, this question should be no trouble.

The first question only required you to work with one of the graphs. Harder questions will require you to find information on one graph and then use it to locate information on the second chart or graph.

CONCLUSION

Graph problems can be tricky. To maximize your chances of getting these questions right, take a few seconds to examine the graphs, noting their titles and scales. This will ensure that you read the right information from the right place. Then speed up any calculations you need to perform by eyeballing and estimating.

DATA INTERPRETATION PRACTICE SET

Directions: The questions in this set refer to the data provided. For each question, select the best answer from among those given.

Questions 1–3 are based on the following graphs.

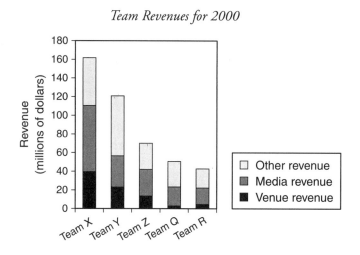

Team Revenues for 2000

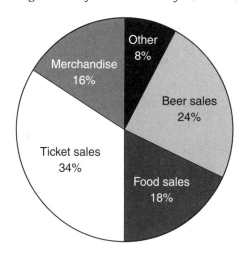

Percentage Source of Venue Revenue for Team X, 2000

1. For the team with the median amount of venue revenue for 2000, media revenue represents approximately what percent of that team's total revenue for that year?

   ○ 25%

   team z

   ○ 30%

   ⊗ 40%

   ○ 55%

   ○ 60%

2. Ticket sales represent approximately what percent of total revenue for Team X in 2000?

   ○ 4%

   ⊗ 8%

   ○ 13%

   ○ 34%

   ○ 54%

3. If Team Y earned total revenue of $150 million in 2001, Team Y's total revenue increased by approximately what percent from 2000 to 2001?

   ○ 20%

   ⊗ 25%

   ○ 30%

   ○ 35%

   ○ 40%

Questions 4–5 are based on the following graph.

Precipitation for County Q, 1995–1999 (inclusive)

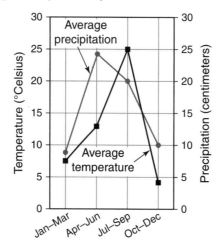

4. Approximately what percent of the total precipitation for Country Q from 1995–1999 fell in the quarter in which the ratio of precipitation to temperature in Celsius was the greatest?

   ⊘ 16%

   ◯ 24%

   ◯ 38%

   ◯ 46%

   ◯ 71%

5. If a drought occurred in 1999 so that the average monthly precipitation for that year was 2.5 centimeters, what was the average yearly precipitation, in centimeters, for 1995–1998 inclusive?

   ◯ 61.5

   ◯ 65.5

   ⊘ 71.3

   ◯ 83.3

   ◯ 95

Questions 6–7 are based on the following graph.

U.S. Health Care Expenditures

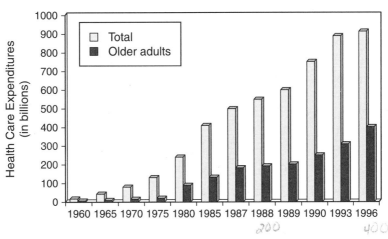

6. What was the increase, in billions of dollars, in health care expenditures by older adults from 1988 to 1996?

   ◯ 160

   ⊗ 210

   ◯ 290

   ◯ 360

   ◯ 400

7. By what percent did total health care expenditures increase from 1980 to 1990?

   ◯ 50%

   ◯ 75%

   ◯ 100%

   ⊗ 200%

   ◯ 300%

ANSWERS AND EXPLANATIONS

1. (C)

Before you get started answering this or any graph question, begin by examining all of the graphs. Here you have two graphs, a segmented bar graph representing team revenue breakdowns for five teams and a pie chart showing the distribution of venue revenues for Team X.

Now you're ready to attack the question, which asks you to find the team with the median venue revenue for 2000 and to determine what percent of that team's revenues is represented by media revenue. This question must refer to the first graph. Therefore, the first part of question—finding the team with the "median" venue revenue—is a simple matter. *Median* refers to the value in the middle, and the venue revenue is represented by the black segment on the bottom of the bar. Here it's clear that the middle value for venue revenue is in the bar in the middle of the graph, so the question clearly refers to Team Z.

The fastest approach to the answer here (and throughout graph questions generally) involves approximating. The downside to bar graphs is that it's often very hard to get a read on the values. The upside is that if you approximate, often you don't have to read the values. Here we need to determine what percent of the bar is represented by media revenue (the dark gray segment in the middle of the bar—always be especially careful to isolate the correct piece of data). By approximating, you should be able to see that the middle segment is more than a third and less than a half of the entire bar. Thus, the correct answer has to be between 33 percent and 50 percent. The only answer that works is (C), 40 percent.

2. (B)

The pie chart tells you that ticket sales represent 34 percent of venue revenue for team X in 2000. Looking at the bar chart, you can see that venue revenue accounted for about $40 million of the $160 million in revenue for team X. That is, venue revenue accounted for about 25 percent of all revenue, and ticket sales 34 percent of this. That's close to one-third of 25 percent, or about 8 percent.

3. (B)

Percent change problems are extremely popular graph questions, and as long as you know how to set them up, they're generally quite easy to answer. This question asks for the approximate percent increase in Team Y's total revenue from 2000 to 2001, so you need to figure out (approximately) the amount of increase, place that over the original (or smaller) amount, and then convert the fraction into a percent.

They give you the total revenue for 2001 as $150 million, so you just need to locate the total revenue for 2000 from the bar graph. It appears to be approximately $120 million, so the amount of increase is $30 million, and the original (or smaller) amount is $120 million. Now apply the formula:

$$\text{Percent increase} \frac{\text{Amount of increase}}{\text{Original (the smaller) amount}} \times 100\% = \frac{\$30 \text{ million}}{\$120 \text{ million}} \times 100\% = 25\%.$$

4. (A)

You can't judge the degree of difficulty of a set of graph questions from the amount of data presented in the graph(s). Here, the graph (really two graphs merged into one field) presents only eight pieces of data, but the questions are surprisingly tricky and the data can be very easy to misinterpret.

The ability to approximate is essential in this question. First, you have to figure out which quarter saw the greatest ratio of precipitation to temperature in Celsius. You should be able to determine this by eyeballing alone. Comparing the precipitation (round point) to the temperature Celsius (square point) for each quarter, it's easy to eliminate the Jul–Sep and Jan–Mar quarters, where the points fall close together. Between the remaining quarters, it looks like the ratio for Apr–Jun is slightly less than 2 to 1, whereas the ratio for Oct–Dec is considerably more than 2 to 1, so the quarter that saw the greatest ratio of precipitation to temperature was Oct–Dec.

Now you simply have to determine what percent of the total annual precipitation for County Q fell during that quarter. Find the sum of all the average precipitations to get the annual average precipitation: 10 + 25 + 20 + 10 = 65 centimeters per year (it's actually closer to 63, but close should be good enough for graph questions). The precipitation that fell in Oct–Dec is around 10, so you just have to find what percent 10 is of 65—or do you? Ten is obviously a lot less than a third of 65, so (**C**), (**D**), and **(E)** are out. If you can see that 10 is less than 20 percent of 65, (10 is 20 percent of 50, so it must be less than 20 percent of 65) then the only possible correct answer is **(A)**, 16 percent.

5. (C)

This is about as tough as it gets on graph problems. You should decide whether to guess and move on or to invest the time it will take to solve the problem. If you decide to guess, you should first try to eliminate some answer choices you know are wrong. You know that 1999 was a drought year, so presumably the average annual precipitation, after 1999 is removed, will be higher. In the last question, you calculated that the average annual precipitation for 1995–1999 was about 65 centimeters. Therefore, the correct answer must be greater than this. Eliminate **(A)** and **(B)** and guess from among the remaining answer choices.

If you decide to calculate an answer, be careful and take it one step at time. The average precipitation for 1995 to 1998 will be the total precipitation over those four years, divided by the number of years from 1995 to 1998, which is 4.

The information in the graph allows you to calculate the total precipitation between 1995 and 1999, and the information in the question allows you to calculate the total precipitation in 1999. Subtract the latter from the former to find the total precipitation from 1995 to 1998.

To determine the total precipitation from 1995 to 1999, add all the quarterly precipitation to get the average precipitation in a year, and then multiply that by the total number of years in the period to get the total precipitation over that period of time. Add 10 + 25 + 20 + 10 = 65 centimeters precipitation per year. That was the average over a five-year period, so total precipitation would be 65 × 5 = 325 centimeters.

To determine the total precipitation for 1999, take the average monthly precipitation for that year and multiply it by 12. You are told that the average monthly precipitation for the drought year was 2.5 centimeters, so the total precipitation for that year is 2.5 × 12 = 30 centimeters for 1999.

Now, to calculate the average annual rainfall for years 1995–1998, subtract the total rainfall for 1999 (30 centimeters) from the total rainfall for all five years (325 centimeters): 325 – 30 = 295. Divide this by 4 to get the average annual rainfall for those years: 295 ÷ 4 is a little less than 75, which is closest to **(C)**.

6. (B)

As always, before you try answering the question, examine the graph. In this case the graphs are a bar graph detailing U.S. health care expenditures for everyone and, to the right, a paired separate bar for older adults from 1960 to 1996. There are a lot of bars represented, so one of the biggest challenges in answering these questions will be to refer to the correct bar.

The question asks for the increase in health care expenditures by older adults from 1988 to 1996. Once again, approximation is the way to go. Another helpful trick for reading bar graphs is to take a sheet of scrap paper and hold it horizontally against the computer screen so that you can more easily read the bar values against the scale. If you do that you should be able to see that in 1988, health care expenditures by older adults were around $200 billion and, in 1996, expenditures by older adults were around $400 billion. Therefore, the increase was around $200 billion, and the closest answer choice is **(B)**, 210.

7. (D)

Yet again, the greatest challenge in answering this question is to get a good reading on the data. Grab a piece of scrap paper and try to come up with approximate figures for total expenditures in 1980 and 1990. Perhaps you'll come up with around $230 billion for 1980 and around $730 billion for 1990. Now apply these numbers to the percent increase formula:

$$\text{Percent increase} = \frac{\text{Amount of increase}}{\text{Original (the smaller) amount}} \times 100\%$$

$$= \frac{500}{230} \times 100\%$$

$$\approx \frac{500}{250} \times 100\%$$

$$= 200\%$$

Part Four

GRE RESOURCES

KAPLAN'S WORD GROUPS

The following lists contain a lot of common GRE words grouped by meaning. Make flashcards from these lists and look over your cards a few times a week from now until Test Day. Look over the word group lists once or twice a week for 30 seconds every week until the test. If you don't have much time until the exam date, look over your lists more frequently. Then, by the day of the test, you should have a rough idea of what most of the words on your lists mean.

Note: The categories in which these words are listed are *general* and should *not* be interpreted as the exact definitions of the words.

ABBREVIATED COMMUNICATION

abridge
compendium
cursory
curtail
syllabus
synopsis
terse

ACT QUICKLY

apace
abrupt
headlong
impetuous
precipitate

ASSIST

abet
advocate
ancillary
bolster
corroborate
countenance
espouse
mainstay
munificent
proponent
stalwart
sustenance

BAD MOOD

bilious
dudgeon
irascible
pettish
petulant
pique
querulous
umbrage
waspish

BEGINNER/AMATEUR

dilettante
fledgling
neophyte
novitiate
proselyte
tyro

BEGINNING/YOUNG

burgeoning
callow
engender
inchoate
incipient
nascent

BITING (AS IN WIT OR TEMPERAMENT)

acerbic
acidulous
acrimonious
asperity
caustic
mordacious
mordant
trenchant

BOLD

audacious
courageous
dauntless

BORING

banal
fatuous
hackneyed
insipid
mundane
pedestrian
platitude
prosaic

quotidian
trite

CAROUSAL

bacchanalian
debauchery
depraved
dissipated
iniquity
libertine
libidinous
licentious
reprobate
ribald
salacious
sordid
turpitude

CHANGING QUICKLY

capricious
mercurial
volatile

COPY

counterpart
emulate
facsimile
factitious
paradigm
precursor
quintessence
simulated
vicarious

CRITICIZE/CRITICISM

aspersion
belittle
berate
calumny
castigate
decry
defamation

denounce
deride/derisive
diatribe
disparage
excoriate
gainsay
harangue
impugn
inveigh
lambaste
objurgate
obloquy
opprobrium
pillory
rebuke
remonstrate
reprehend
reprove
revile
tirade
vituperate

DEATH/MOURNING
bereave
cadaver
defunct
demise
dolorous
elegy
knell
lament
macabre
moribund
obsequies
sepulchral
wraith

DENYING OF SELF
abnegate
abstain
ascetic
spartan

stoic
temperate

DICTATORIAL
authoritarian
despotic
dogmatic
hegemonic/hegemony
imperious
peremptory
tyrannical

DIFFICULT TO UNDERSTAND
abstruse
ambiguous
arcane
bemusing
cryptic
enigmatic
esoteric
inscrutable
obscure
opaque
paradoxical
perplexing
recondite
turbid

DISGUSTING/OFFENSIVE
defile
fetid
invidious
noisome
odious
putrid
rebarbative

EASY TO UNDERSTAND
articulate
cogent
eloquent

evident
limpid
lucid
pellucid

ECCENTRIC/DISSIMILAR
aberrant
anachronism
anomalous
discrete
eclectic
esoteric
iconoclast

EMBARRASS
abash
chagrin
compunction
contrition
diffidence
expiate
foible
gaucherie
rue

EQUAL
equitable
equity
tantamount

FALSEHOOD
apocryphal
canard
chicanery
dissemble
duplicity
equivocate
erroneous
ersatz
fallacious
feigned
guile

mendacious/
   mendacity
perfidy
prevaricate
specious
spurious

FAMILY
conjugal
consanguine
distaff
endogamous
filial
fratricide
progenitor
scion

FAVORING/NOT IMPARTIAL
ardor/ardent
doctrinaire
fervid
partisan
tendentious
zealot

FORGIVE
absolve
acquit
exculpate
exonerate
expiate
palliate
redress
vindicate

FUNNY
chortle
droll
facetious
flippant
gibe

jocular
levity
ludicrous
raillery
riposte
simper

GAPS/OPENINGS
abatement
aperture
fissure
hiatus
interregnum
interstice
lull
orifice
rent
respite
rift

GENEROUS/KIND
altruistic
beneficent
clement
largess
magnanimous
munificent
philanthropic
unstinting

GREEDY
avaricious
covetous
mercenary
miserly
penurious
rapacious
venal

HARDHEARTED
asperity
baleful

dour
fell
malevolent
mordant
sardonic
scathing
truculent
vitriolic
vituperation

HARMFUL
baleful
baneful
deleterious
inimical
injurious
insidious
minatory
perfidious
pernicious

HARSH-SOUNDING
cacophony
din
dissonant
raucous
strident

HATRED
abhorrence
anathema
antagonism
antipathy
detestation
enmity
loathing
malice
odium
rancor

HEALTHY
beneficial

salubrious
salutary

HESITATE
dither
oscillate
teeter
vacillate
waver

HOSTILE
antithetic
churlish
curmudgeon
irascible
malevolent
misanthropic
truculent
vindictive

INNOCENT/ INEXPERIENCED
credulous
gullible
ingenuous
naive
novitiate
tyro

INSINCERE
disingenuous
dissemble
fulsome
ostensible
unctuous

INVESTIGATE
appraise
ascertain
assay
descry
peruse

LAZY/SLUGGISH
indolent
inert
lackadaisical
languid
lassitude
lethargic
phlegmatic
quiescent
slothful
torpid

LUCK
adventitious
amulet
auspicious
fortuitous
kismet
optimum
portentous
propitiate
propitious
providential
talisman

NAG
admonish
cavil
belabor
enjoin
exhort
harangue
hector
martinet
remonstrate
reproof

NASTY
fetid
noisome
noxious

NOT A STRAIGHT LINE
askance
awry
careen
carom
circuitous
circumvent
gyrate
labyrinth
meander
oblique
serrated
sidle
sinuous
undulating
vortex

OVERBLOWN/WORDY
bombastic
circumlocution
garrulous
grandiloquent
loquacious
periphrastic
prolix
rhetoric
turgid
verbose

PACIFY/SATISFY
ameliorate
appease
assuage
defer
mitigate
mollify
placate
propitiate
satiate
slake
sooth

PLEASANT-SOUNDING

euphonious
harmonious
melodious
sonorous

POOR

destitute
esurient
impecunious
indigent

PRAISE

acclaim
accolade
aggrandize
encomium
eulogize
extol
fawn
laud/laudatory
venerate/veneration

PREDICT

augur
auspice
fey
harbinger
portentous
presage
prescient
prognosticate

PREVENT/OBSTRUCT

discomfort
encumber
fetter
forfend
hinder
impede
inhibit
occlude

SMART/LEARNED

astute
canny
erudite
perspicacious

SORROW

disconsolate
doleful
dolor
elegiac
forlorn
lament
lugubrious
melancholy
morose
plaintive
threnody

STUBBORN

implacable
inexorable
intractable
intransigent
obdurate
obstinate
recalcitrant
refractory
renitent
untoward
vexing

TERSE

compendious
curt
laconic
pithy
succinct
taciturn

TIME/ORDER/DURATION

anachronism

antecede
antedate
anterior
archaic
diurnal
eon
ephemeral
epoch
fortnight
millennium
penultimate
synchronous
temporal

TIMID/TIMIDITY

craven
diffident
pusillanimous
recreant
timorous
trepidation

TRUTH

candor/candid
fealty
frankness
indisputable
indubitable
legitimate
probity
sincere
veracious
verity

UNUSUAL

aberration
anomaly
iconoclast
idiosyncrasy

WALKING ABOUT

ambulatory

itinerant
peripatetic

WANDERING
discursive
expatiate
forage
itinerant
peregrination
peripatetic
sojourn

WEAKEN
adulterate
enervate
exacerbate
inhibit
obviate

stultify
undermine
vitiate

WISDOM
adage
aphorism
apothegm
axiom
bromide
dictum
epigram
platitude
sententious
truism

WITHDRAWAL/RETREAT
abeyance

abjure
abnegation
abortive
abrogate
decamp
demur
recant
recidivism
remission
renege
rescind
retrograde

KAPLAN'S ROOT LIST

Kaplan's Root List can boost your knowledge of GRE-level words, and that can help you get more questions right. No one can predict exactly which words will show up on your test, but there are certain words that the test makers favor. The Root List gives you the component parts of many typical GRE words. Knowing these words can help you because you may run across them on your GRE. Also, becoming comfortable with the types of words that pop up will reduce your anxiety about the test.

Knowing roots can help you in two more ways. First, instead of learning one word at a time, you can learn a whole group of words that contain a certain root. They'll be related in meaning, so if you remember one, it will be easier for you to remember others. Second, roots can often help you decode an unknown GRE word. If you recognize a familiar root, you could get a good enough grasp of the word to answer the question.

A: WITHOUT

amoral: neither moral nor immoral
atheist: one who does not believe in God
atypical: not typical
anonymous: of unknown authorship or origin
apathy: lack of interest or emotion
atrophy: the wasting away of body tissue
anomaly: an irregularity
agnostic: one who questions the existence of God

AB/ABS: OFF, AWAY FROM, APART, DOWN

abduct: to take by force
abhor: to hate, detest
abolish: to do away with, make void
abstract: conceived apart from concrete realities, specific objects, or actual instances
abnormal: deviating from a standard
abdicate: to renounce or relinquish a throne
abstinence: forbearance from any indulgence of appetite
abstruse: hard to understand; secret, hidden

AC/ACR: SHARP, BITTER

acid: something that is sharp, sour, or ill natured
acute: sharp at the end; ending in a point
acerbic: sour or astringent in taste; harsh in temper
acrid: sharp or biting to the taste or smell
acrimonious: caustic, stinging, or bitter in nature
exacerbate: to increase bitterness or violence; aggravate

ACT/AG: TO DO; TO DRIVE; TO FORCE; TO LEAD

agile: quick and well-coordinated in movement; active, lively
agitate: to move or force into violent, irregular action
litigate: to make the subject of a lawsuit
prodigal: wastefully or recklessly extravagant
pedagogue: a teacher
synagogue: a gathering or congregation of Jews for the purpose of religious worship

AD/AL: TO, TOWARD, NEAR

adapt: adjust or modify fittingly
adjacent: near, close, or contiguous; adjoining
addict: to give oneself over, as to a habit or pursuit
admire: to regard with wonder, pleasure, and approval
address: to direct a speech or written statement to

adhere: to stick fast; cleave; cling

adjoin: to be close or in contact with

advocate: to plead in favor of

AL/ALI/ALTER: OTHER, ANOTHER

alternative: a possible choice

alias: an assumed name; another name

alibi: the defense by an accused person that he was verifiably elsewhere at the time of the crime with which he is charged

alien: one born in another country; a foreigner

alter ego: the second self; a substitute or deputy

altruist: a person unselfishly concerned for the welfare of others

allegory: figurative treatment of one subject under the guise of another

AM: LOVE

amateur: a person who engages in an activity for pleasure rather than financial or professional gain

amatory: of or pertaining to lovers or lovemaking

amenity: agreeable ways or manners

amorous: inclined to love, esp. sexual love

enamored: inflamed with love; charmed; captivated

amity: friendship; peaceful harmony

inamorata: a female lover

amiable: having or showing agreeable personal qualities

amicable: characterized by exhibiting good will

AMB: TO GO; TO WALK

ambient: moving freely; circulating

ambitious: desirous of achieving or obtaining power

preamble: an introductory statement

ambassador: an authorized messenger or representative

ambulance: a wheeled vehicle equipped for carrying sick people, usually to a hospital

ambulatory: of, pertaining to, or capable of walking

ambush: the act of lying concealed so as to attack by surprise

perambulator: one who makes a tour of inspection on foot

AMBI/AMPH: BOTH, MORE THAN ONE, AROUND

ambiguous: open to various interpretations

amphibian: any cold-blooded vertebrate, the larva of which is aquatic and the adult of which is terrestrial; a person or thing having a twofold nature

ambidextrous: able to use both hands equally well

ANIM: OF THE LIFE, MIND, SOUL, SPIRIT

unanimous: in complete accord
animosity: a feeling of ill will or enmity
animus: hostile feeling or attitude
equanimity: mental or emotional stability, especially under tension
magnanimous: generous in forgiving an insult or injury

ANNUI/ENNI: YEAR

annual: of, for, or pertaining to a year; yearly
anniversary: the yearly recurrence of the date of a past event
annuity: a specified income payable at stated intervals
perennial: lasting for an indefinite amount of time
annals: a record of events, esp. a yearly record

ANTE: BEFORE

anterior: placed before
antecedent: existing, being, or going before
antedate: precede in time
antebellum: before the war (especially the American Civil War)
antediluvian: belonging to the period before the biblical flood; very old or
    old-fashioned

ANTHRO/ANDR: MAN, HUMAN

anthropology: the science that deals with the origins of humankind
android: robot; mechanical human
misanthrope: one who hates humans or humankind
philanderer: one who carries on flirtations
androgynous: being both male and female
androgen: any substance that promotes masculine characteristics
anthropocentric: regarding humanity as the central fact of the universe

ANTI: AGAINST

antibody: a protein naturally existing in blood serum that reacts to overcome the
    toxic effects of an antigen
antidote: a remedy for counteracting the effects of poison, disease, etc.
antiseptic: free from germs; particularly clean or neat
antipathy: aversion
antipodal: on the opposite side of the globe

APO: AWAY

apology: an expression of one's regret or sorrow for having wronged another
apostle: one of the 12 disciples sent forth by Jesus to preach the gospel

apocalypse: revelation; discovery; disclosure
apogee: the highest or most distant point
apocryphal: of doubtful authorship or authenticity
apostasy: a total desertion of one's religion, principles, party, cause, etc.

ARCH/ARCHI/ARCHY: CHIEF, PRINCIPAL, RULER

architect: the devisor, maker, or planner of anything
archenemy: chief enemy
monarchy: a government in which the supreme power is lodged in a sovereign
anarchy: a state or society without government or law
oligarchy: a state or society ruled by a select group

AUTO: SELF

automatic: self-moving or self-acting
autocrat: an absolute ruler
autonomy: independence or freedom

BE: TO BE; TO HAVE A PARTICULAR QUALITY; TO EXIST

belittle: to regard something as less impressive than it apparently is
bemoan: to express pity for
bewilder: to confuse or puzzle completely
belie: to misrepresent; to contradict

BEL/BELL: WAR

antebellum: before the war
rebel: a person who resists authority, control, or tradition
belligerent: warlike, given to waging war

BEN/BON: GOOD

benefit: anything advantageous to a person or thing
benign: having a kindly disposition
benediction: act of uttering a blessing
benevolent: desiring to do good to others
bonus: something given over and above what is due
bona fide: in good faith; without fraud

BI: TWICE, DOUBLE

binocular: involving two eyes
biennial: happening every two years
bilateral: pertaining to or affecting two or both sides
bilingual: able to speak one's native language and another with equal facility
bipartisan: representing two parties

CAD/CID: TO FALL; TO HAPPEN BY CHANCE

accident: happening by chance; unexpected

coincidence: a striking occurrence of two or more events at one time, apparently by chance

decadent: decaying; deteriorating

cascade: a waterfall descending over a steep surface

recidivist: one who repeatedly relapses, as into crime

CANT/CENT/CHANT: TO SING

accent: prominence of a syllable in terms of pronunciation

chant: a song; singing

enchant: to subject to magical influence; bewitch

recant: to withdraw or disavow a statement

incantation: the chanting of words purporting to have magical power

incentive: that which incites action

CAP/CIP/CEPT: TO TAKE; TO GET

capture: to take by force or stratagem

anticipate: to realize beforehand; foretaste or foresee

susceptible: capable of receiving, admitting, undergoing, or being affected by something

emancipate: to free from restraint

percipient: having perception; discerning; discriminating

precept: a commandment or direction given as a rule of conduct

CAP/CAPIT/CIPIT: HEAD, HEADLONG

capital: the city or town that is the official seat of government

disciple: one who is a pupil of the doctrines of another

precipitate: to hasten the occurrence of; to bring about prematurely

precipice: a cliff with a vertical face

capitulate: to surrender unconditionally or on stipulated terms

caption: a heading or title

CARD/CORD/COUR: HEART

cardiac: pertaining to the heart

encourage: to inspire with spirit or confidence

concord: agreement; peace, amity

discord: lack of harmony between persons or things

concordance: agreement, concord, harmony

CARN: FLESH

carnivorous: eating flesh
carnage: the slaughter of a great number of people
carnival: a traveling amusement show
reincarnation: rebirth of a soul in a new body
incarnation: a being invested with a bodily form

CAST/CHAST: CUT

cast: to throw or hurl; fling
caste: a hereditary social group, limited to people of the same rank
castigate: to punish in order to correct
chastise: to discipline, esp. by corporal punishment
chaste: free from obscenity; decent

CED/CEED/CESS: TO GO; TO YIELD; TO STOP

antecedent: existing, being, or going before
concede: to acknowledge as true, just, or proper; admit
predecessor: one who comes before another in an office, position, etc.
cessation: a temporary or complete discontinuance
incessant: without stop

CENTR: CENTER

concentrate: to bring to a common center; to converge, to direct toward one point
eccentric: off center
concentric: having a common center, as in circles or spheres
centrifuge: an apparatus that rotates at high speed to separate substances of
    different densities using centrifugal force
centrist: of or pertaining to moderate political or social ideas

CERN/CERT/CRET/CRIM/CRIT: TO SEPARATE; TO JUDGE; TO DISTINGUISH; TO DECIDE

discrete: detached from others, separate
ascertain: to make sure of; to determine
certitude: freedom from doubt
discreet: judicious in one's conduct of speech, esp. with regard to maintaining
    silence about something of a delicate nature
hypocrite: a person who pretends to have beliefs that she does not
criterion: a standard of judgment or criticism

CHRON: TIME

synchronize: to occur at the same time or agree in time
chronology: the sequential order in which past events occurred

anachronism: an obsolete or archaic form

chronic: constant, habitual

chronometer: a time piece with a mechanism to adjust for accuracy

CIRCU: AROUND, ON ALL SIDES

circumference: the outer boundary of a circular area

circumstances: the existing conditions or state of affairs surrounding and affecting an agent

circuit: the act of going or moving around

circumambulate: to walk about or around

circuitous: roundabout, indirect

CIS: TO CUT

scissors: cutting instrument for paper

precise: definitely stated or defined

exorcise: to seek to expel an evil spirit by ceremony

incision: a cut, gash, or notch

incisive: penetrating, cutting

CLA/CLO/CLU: SHUT, CLOSE

conclude: to bring to an end; finish; to terminate

claustrophobia: an abnormal fear of enclosed places

disclose: to make known, reveal, or uncover

exclusive: not admitting of something else; shutting out others

cloister: a courtyard bordered with covered walks, esp. in a religious institution

preclude: to prevent the presence, existence, or occurrence of

CLAIM/CLAM: TO SHOUT; TO CRY OUT

exclaim: to cry out or speak suddenly and vehemently

proclaim: to announce or declare in an official way

clamor: a loud uproar

disclaim: to deny interest in or connection with

reclaim: to claim or demand the return of a right or possession

CLI: TO LEAN TOWARD

decline: to cause to slope or incline downward

recline: to lean back

climax: the most intense point in the development of something

proclivity: inclination, bias

disinclination: aversion, distaste

CO/COL/COM/CON: WITH, TOGETHER

connect: to bind or fasten together
coerce: to compel by force, intimidation, or authority
compatible: capable of existing together in harmony
collide: to strike one another with a forceful impact
collaborate: to work with another, cooperate
conciliate: to placate, win over
commensurate: suitable in measure, proportionate

COUR/CUR: RUNNING; A COURSE

recur: to happen again
curriculum: the regular course of study
courier: a messenger traveling in haste who bears news
excursion: a short journey or trip
cursive: handwriting in flowing strokes with the letters joined together
concur: to accord in opinion; agree
incursion: a hostile entrance into a place, esp. suddenly
cursory: going rapidly over something; hasty; superficial

CRE/CRESC/CRET: TO GROW

accrue: to be added as a matter of periodic gain
creation: the act of producing or causing to exist
increase: to make greater in any respect
increment: something added or gained; an addition or increase
accretion: an increase by natural growth

CRED: TO BELIEVE; TO TRUST

incredible: unbelievable
credentials: anything that provides the basis for belief
credo: any formula of belief
credulity: willingness to believe or trust too readily
credit: trustworthiness

CRYP: HIDDEN

crypt: a subterranean chamber or vault
apocryphal: of doubtful authorship or authenticity
cryptology: the science of interpreting secret writings, codes, ciphers, and the like
cryptography: procedures of making and using secret writing

CUB/CUMB: TO LIE DOWN

cubicle: any small space or compartment that is partitioned off
succumb: to give away to superior force; yield
incubate: to sit upon for the purpose of hatching
incumbent: holding an indicated position
recumbent: lying down; reclining; leaning

CULP: BLAME

culprit: a person guilty for an offense
culpable: deserving blame or censure
inculpate: to charge with fault
mea culpa: through my fault; my fault

DAC/DOC: TO TEACH

doctor: someone licensed to practice medicine; a learned person
doctrine: a particular principle advocated, as of a government or religion
indoctrinate: to imbue a person with learning
docile: easily managed or handled; tractable
didactic: intended for instruction

DE: AWAY, OFF, DOWN, COMPLETELY, REVERSAL

descend: to move from a higher to a lower place
decipher: to make out the meaning; to interpret
defile: to make foul, dirty, or unclean
defame: to attack the good name or reputation of
deferential: respectful; to yield to judgment
delineate: to trace the outline of; sketch or trace in outline

DEM: PEOPLE

democracy: government by the people
epidemic: affecting at the same time a large number of people and spreading from person to person
endemic: peculiar to a particular people or locality
pandemic: general, universal
demographics: vital and social statistics of populations

DI/DIA: APART, THROUGH

dialogue: conversation between two or more persons
diagnose: to determine the identity of something from the symptoms
dilate: to make wider or larger; to cause to expand
dilatory: inclined to delay or procrastinate
dichotomy: division into two parts, kinds, etc.

DIC/DICT/DIT: TO SAY; TO TELL; TO USE WORDS

dictionary: a book containing a selection of the words of a language
predict: to tell in advance
verdict: judgment, decree
interdict: to forbid; prohibit

DIGN: WORTH

dignity: nobility or elevation of character; worthiness
dignitary: a person who holds a high rank or office
deign: to think fit or in accordance with one's dignity
condign: well deserved; fitting; adequate
disdain: to look upon or treat with contempt

DIS/DIF: AWAY FROM, APART, REVERSAL, NOT

disperse: to drive or send off in various directions
disseminate: to scatter or spread widely; promulgate
dissipate: to scatter wastefully
dissuade: to deter by advice or persuasion
diffuse: to pour out and spread, as in a fluid

DOG/DOX: OPINION

orthodox: sound or correct in opinion or doctrine
paradox: an opinion or statement contrary to accepted opinion
dogma: a system of tenets, as of a church

DOL: SUFFER, PAIN

condolence: expression of sympathy with one who is suffering
indolence: a state of being lazy or slothful
doleful: sorrowful, mournful
dolorous: full of pain or sorrow, grievous

DON/DOT/DOW: TO GIVE

donate: to present as a gift or contribution
pardon: kind indulgence, forgiveness
antidote: something that prevents or counteracts ill effects
anecdote: a short narrative about an interesting event
endow: to provide with a permanent fund

DUB: DOUBT

dubious: doubtful
dubiety: doubtfulness
indubitable: unquestionable

DUC/DUCT: TO LEAD

abduct: to carry off or lead away
conduct: personal behavior, way of acting
conducive: contributive, helpful
induce: to lead or move by influence
induct: to install in a position with formal ceremonies
produce: to bring into existence; give cause to

DUR: HARD

endure: to hold out against; to sustain without yielding
durable: able to resist decay
duress: compulsion by threat, coercion
dour: sullen, gloomy
duration: the length of time something exists

DYS: FAULTY, ABNORMAL

dystrophy: faulty or inadequate nutrition or development
dyspepsia: impaired digestion
dyslexia: an impairment of the ability to read due to a brain defect
dysfunctional: poorly functioning

E/EF/EX: OUT, OUT OF, FROM, FORMER, COMPLETELY

evade: to escape from, avoid
exclude: to shut out; to leave out
extricate: to disentangle, release
exonerate: to free or declare free from blame
expire: to come to an end; to cease to be valid
efface: to rub or wipe out; to surpass, eclipse

EPI: UPON

epidemic: affecting at the same time a large number of people and spreading from
  person to person
epilogue: a concluding part added to a literary work
epidermis: the outer layer of the skin
epigram: a witty or pointed saying tersely expressed
epithet: a word or phrase, used invectively as a term of abuse

EQU: EQUAL, EVEN

equation: the act of making equal
adequate: equal to the requirement or occasion
equidistant: equally distant
iniquity: gross injustice; wickedness

ERR: TO WANDER

err: to go astray in thought or belief, to be mistaken
error: a deviation from accuracy or correctness
erratic: deviating from the proper or usual course in conduct
arrant: downright, thorough, notorious

ESCE: BECOMING

adolescent: between childhood and adulthood
obsolescent: becoming obsolete
incandescent: glowing with heat, shining
convalescent: recovering from illness
reminiscent: reminding or suggestive of

EU: GOOD, WELL

euphemism: pleasant-sounding term for something unpleasant
eulogy: speech or writing in praise or commendation
eugenics: improvement of qualities of race by control of inherited characteristics
euthanasia: killing a person painlessly, usually one who has an incurable,
    painful disease
euphony: pleasantness of sound

EXTRA: OUTSIDE, BEYOND

extraordinary: beyond the ordinary
extract: to take out, obtain against a person's will
extradite: to hand over (person accused of crime) to the state where crime was
    committed
extrasensory: derived by means other than known senses
extrapolate: to estimate (unknown facts or values) from known data

FAB/FAM: SPEAK

fable: fictional tale, esp. legendary
affable: friendly, courteous
ineffable: too great for description in words; that which must not be uttered
famous: well known, celebrated
defame: attack good name of

FAC/FIC/FIG/FAIT/FEIT/FY: TO DO; TO MAKE

factory: building for manufacture of goods
faction: small dissenting group within larger one, esp. in politics
deficient: incomplete or insufficient
prolific: producing many offspring or much output
configuration: manner of arrangement, shape

ratify: to confirm or accept by formal consent
effigy: sculpture or model of person
counterfeit: imitation, forgery

FER: TO BRING; TO CARRY; TO BEAR

offer: to present for acceptance, refusal, or consideration
confer: to grant, bestow
referendum: to vote on political question open to the entire electorate
proffer: to offer
proliferate: to reproduce; produce rapidly

FERV: TO BOIL; TO BUBBLE

fervor: passion, zeal
fervid: ardent, intense
effervescent: with the quality of giving off bubbles of gas

FID: FAITH, TRUST

confide: to entrust with a secret
affidavit: written statement on oath
fidelity: faithfulness, loyalty
fiduciary: of a trust; held or given in trust
infidel: disbeliever in the supposed true religion

FIN: END

final: at the end; coming last
confine: to keep or restrict within certain limits; imprison
definitive: decisive, unconditional, final
infinite: boundless; endless
infinitesimal: infinitely or very small

FLAG/FLAM: TO BURN

flammable: easily set on fire
flambeau: a lighted torch
flagrant: blatant, scandalous
conflagration: a large, destructive fire

FLECT/FLEX: TO BEND

deflect: to bend or turn aside from a purpose
flexible: able to bend without breaking
inflect: to change or vary pitch of
reflect: to throw back
genuflect: to bend knee, esp. in worship

FLU/FLUX: TO FLOW

fluid: substance, esp. gas or liquid, capable of flowing freely
fluctuation: something that varies, rising and falling
effluence: flowing out of (light, electricity, etc.)
confluence: merging into one
mellifluous: pleasing, musical

FORE: BEFORE

foresight: care or provision for the future
foreshadow: be a warning or indication of (future event)
forestall: to prevent by advance action
forthright: straightforward, outspoken, decisive

FORT: CHANCE

fortune: chance or luck in human affairs
fortunate: lucky, auspicious
fortuitous: happening by luck

FORT: STRENGTH

fortify: to provide with fortifications; strengthen
fortissimo: very loud
forte: strong point; something a person does well

FRA/FRAC/FRAG/FRING: TO BREAK

fracture: breakage, esp. of a bone
fragment: a part broken off
fractious: irritable, peevish
refractory: stubborn, unmanageable, rebellious
infringe: to break or violate (law, etc.)

FUS: TO POUR

profuse: lavish, extravagant, copious
fusillade: continuous discharge of firearms or outburst of criticism
suffuse: to spread throughout or over from within
diffuse: to spread widely or thinly
infusion: infusing; liquid extract so obtained

GEN: BIRTH, CREATION, RACE, KIND

generous: giving or given freely
genetics: study of heredity and variation among animals and plants
gender: classification roughly corresponding to the two sexes and sexlessness
carcinogenic: producing cancer

congenital: existing or as such from birth
progeny: offspring, descendants
miscegenation: interbreeding of races

GN/GNO: KNOW

agnostic: person who believes that the existence of God is not provable
ignore: to refuse to take notice of
ignoramus: a person lacking knowledge, uninformed
recognize: to identify as already known
incognito: with one's name or identity concealed
prognosis: to forecast, especially of disease
diagnose: to make an identification of disease or fault from symptoms

GRAD/GRESS: TO STEP

progress: forward movement
aggressive: given to hostile act or feeling
degrade: to humiliate, dishonor, reduce to lower rank
digress: to depart from main subject
egress: going out; way out
regress: to move backward, revert to an earlier state

GRAT: PLEASING

grateful: thankful
ingratiate: to bring oneself into favor
gratuity: money given for good service
gracious: kindly, esp. to inferiors; merciful

HER/HES: TO STICK

coherent: logically consistent; having waves in phase and of one wavelength
adhesive: tending to remain in memory; sticky; an adhesive substance
inherent: involved in the constitution or essential character of something
adherent: able to adhere; believer or advocate of a particular thing
heredity: the qualities genetically derived from one's ancestors and the transmission of those qualities

(H)ETERO: DIFFERENT

heterosexual: of or pertaining to sexual orientation toward members of the opposite sex; relating to different sexes
heterogeneous: of other origin; not originating in the body
heterodox: different from acknowledged standard; holding unorthodox opinions or doctrines

(H)OM: SAME

homogeneous: of the same or a similar kind of nature; of uniform structure of composition throughout

homonym: one of two or more words spelled and pronounced alike but different in meaning

homosexual: of, relating to, or exhibiting sexual desire toward a member of one's own sex

anomaly: deviation from the common rule

homeostasis: a relatively stable state of equilibrium

HYPER: OVER, EXCESSIVE

hyperactive: excessively active

hyperbole: purposeful exaggeration for effect

hyperglycemia: an abnormally high concentration of sugar in the blood

HYPO: UNDER, BENEATH, LESS THAN

hypodermic: relating to the parts beneath the skin

hypochondriac: one affected by extreme depression of mind or spirits, often centered on imaginary physical ailments

hypocritical: affecting virtues or qualities one does not have

hypothesis: assumption subject to proof

IDIO: ONE'S OWN

idiot: an utterly stupid person

idiom: a language, dialect, or style of speaking particular to a people

idiosyncrasy: peculiarity of temperament; eccentricity

IM/IN/EM/EN: IN, INTO

embrace: to clasp in the arms; to include or contain

enclose: to close in on all sides

intrinsic: belonging to a thing by its very nature

influx: the act of flowing in; inflow

implicit: not expressly stated; implied

incarnate: given a bodily, esp. a human, form

indigenous: native; innate, natural

IM/IN: NOT, WITHOUT

inactive: not active

innocuous: not harmful or injurious

indolence: showing a disposition to avoid exertion; slothful

impartial: not partial or biased; just

indigent: lacking financial means; impoverished

INTER: BETWEEN, AMONG

interstate: connecting or jointly involving states
interim: a temporary or provisional arrangement; meantime
interloper: one who intrudes in the domain of others
intermittent: stopping or ceasing for a time
intersperse: to scatter here and there

JECT: TO THROW; TO THROW DOWN

inject: to place (quality, etc.) where needed in something
dejected: sad, depressed
eject: to throw out, expel
conjecture: formation of opinion on incomplete information
abject: utterly hopeless, humiliating, or wretched

JOIN/JUNCT: TO MEET; TO JOIN

junction: the act of joining; combining
adjoin: to be next to and joined with
subjugate: to conquer
rejoinder: to reply, retort
junta: (usually military) clique taking power after a coup d'état

JUR: TO SWEAR

perjury: willful lying while under oath
abjure: to renounce under oath
adjure: to beg or command

LAV/LUT/LUV: TO WASH

lavatory: a room with equipment for washing hands and face
dilute: to make thinner or weaker by the addition of water
pollute: to make foul or unclean
deluge: a great flood of water
antediluvian: before the biblical flood; extremely old
ablution: act of cleansing

LECT/LEG: TO SELECT, TO CHOOSE

collect: to gather together or assemble
elect: to choose; to decide
select: to choose with care
eclectic: selecting ideas, etc. from various sources
predilection: preference, liking

LEV: LIFT, LIGHT, RISE

relieve: to mitigate; to free from a burden
alleviate: to make easier to endure, lessen
relevant: bearing on or pertinent to information at hand
levee: embankment against river flooding
levitate: to rise in the air; to cause to rise
levity: humor, frivolity, gaiety

LOC/LOG/LOQU: WORD, SPEECH

dialogue: conversation, esp. in a literary work
elocution: art of clear and expressive speaking
prologue: introduction to poem, play, etc.
eulogy: speech or writing in praise of someone
colloquial: of ordinary or familiar conversation
grandiloquent: pompous or inflated in language
loquacious: talkative

LUC/LUM/LUS: LIGHT

illustrate: to make intelligible with examples or analogies
illuminate: to supply or brighten with light
illustrious: highly distinguished
translucent: permitting light to pass through
lackluster: lacking brilliance or radiance
lucid: easily understood, intelligible
luminous: bright, brilliant, glowing

LUD/LUS: TO PLAY

allude: to refer casually or indirectly
illusion: something that deceives by producing a false impression of reality
ludicrous: ridiculous, laughable
delude: to mislead the mind or judgment of, deceive
elude: to avoid capture or escape defection by
prelude: a preliminary to an action, event, etc.

MAG/MAJ/MAX: BIG

magnify: to increase the apparent size of
magnitude: greatness of size, extent, or dimensions
maximum: the highest amount, value, or degree attained
magnate: a powerful or influential person
magnanimous: generous in forgiving an insult or injury
maxim: an expression of general truth or principle

MAL/MALE: BAD, ILL, EVIL, WRONG

malfunction: failure to function properly
malicious: full of or showing malice
malign: to speak harmful untruths about, to slander
malady: a disorder or disease of the body
maladroit: clumsy, tactless
malapropism: humorous misuse of a word
malfeasance: misconduct or wrongdoing often committed by a public official
malediction: a curse

MAN: HAND

manual: operated by hand
manufacture: to make by hand or machinery
emancipate: to free from bondage
manifest: readily perceived by the eye or the understanding
mandate: an authoritative order or command

MIN: SMALL

minute: a unit of time equal to one-sixtieth of an hour, or sixty seconds
minutiae: small or trivial details
miniature: a copy or model that represents something in greatly reduced size
diminish: to lessen
diminution: the act or process of diminishing

MIN: TO PROJECT, TO HANG OVER

eminent: towering above others; projecting
imminent: about to occur; impending
prominent: projecting outward
preeminent: superior to or notable above all others
minatory: menacing, threatening

MIS/MIT: TO SEND

transmit: to send from one person, thing, or place to another
emissary: a messenger or agent sent to represent the interests of another
intermittent: stopping and starting at intervals
remit: to send money
remission: a lessening of intensity or degree

MISC: MIXED

miscellaneous: made up of a variety of parts or ingredients
miscegenation: the interbreeding of races, esp. marriage between white and
    nonwhite persons
promiscuous: consisting of diverse and unrelated parts or individuals

MON/MONIT: TO REMIND; TO WARN

monument: a structure, such as a building, tower, or sculpture, erected as
   a memorial
monitor: one that admonishes, cautions, or reminds
summon: to call together; convene
admonish: to counsel against something; caution
remonstrate: to say or plead in protect, objection, or reproof
premonition: forewarning, presentiment

MORPH: SHAPE

amorphous: without definite form; lacking a specific shape
metamorphosis: a transformation, as by magic or sorcery
anthropomorphism: attribution of human characteristics to inanimate objects,
   animals, or natural phenomena

MORT: DEATH

immortal: not subject to death
morbid: susceptible to preoccupation with unwholesome matters
moribund: dying, decaying

MUT: CHANGE

commute: to substitute; exchange; interchange
mutation: the process of being changed
transmutation: the act of changing from one form into another
permutation: a complete change; transformation
immutable: unchangeable, invariable

NAT/NAS/NAI: TO BE BORN

natural: present due to nature, not to artificial or man-made means
native: belonging to one by nature; inborn; innate
naive: lacking worldliness and sophistication; artless
cognate: related by blood; having a common ancestor
renaissance: rebirth, esp. referring to culture
nascent: starting to develop

NIC/NOC/NOX: HARM

innocent: uncorrupted by evil, malice, or wrongdoing
noxious: injurious or harmful to health or morals
obnoxious: highly disagreeable or offensive
innocuous: having no adverse effect; harmless

NOM: RULE, ORDER

astronomy: the scientific study of the universe beyond the earth

economy: the careful or thrifty use of resources, as of income, materials, or labor

gastronomy: the art or science of good eating

taxonomy: the science, laws, or principles of classification

autonomy: independence, self-governance

NOM/NYM/NOUN/NOWN: NAME

synonym: a word having a meaning similar to that of another word of the same language

anonymous: having an unknown or unacknowledged name

nominal: existing in name only; negligible

nominate: to propose by name as a candidate

nomenclature: a system of names; systematic naming

acronym: a word formed from the initial letters of a name

NOUNC/NUNC: TO ANNOUNCE

announce: to proclaim

pronounce: to articulate

renounce: to give up, especially by formal announcement

NOV/NEO/NOU: NEW

novice: a person new to any field or activity

renovate: to restore to an earlier condition

innovate: to begin or introduce something new

neologism: a newly coined word, phrase, or expression

neophyte: a recent convert

nouveau riche: one who has lately become rich

OB/OC/OF/OP: TOWARD, TO, AGAINST, OVER

obese: extremely fat, corpulent

obstinate: stubbornly adhering to an idea, inflexible

obstruct: to block or fill with obstacles

oblique: having a slanting or sloping direction

obstreperous: noisily defiant, unruly

obtuse: not sharp, pointed, or acute in any form

obfuscate: to render indistinct or dim; darken

obsequious: overly submissive

OMNI : ALL

omnibus: an anthology of the works of one author or of writings on related subjects
omnipresent: everywhere at one time
omnipotent: all powerful
omniscient: having infinite knowledge

PAC/PEAC: PEACE

appease: to bring peace to
pacify: to ease the anger or agitation of
pacifier: something or someone that eases the anger or agitation of
pact: a formal agreement, as between nations

PAN: ALL, EVERYONE

panorama: an unobstructed and wide view of an extensive area
panegyric: formal or elaborate praise at an assembly
panoply: a wide-ranging and impressive array or display
pantheon: a public building containing tombs or memorials of the illustrious dead
    of a nation
pandemic: widespread, general, universal

PAR: EQUAL

par: an equality in value or standing
parity: equally, as in amount, status, or character
apartheid: any system or caste that separates people according to race, etc.
disparage: to belittle, speak disrespectfully about
disparate: essentially different

PARA: NEXT TO, BESIDE

parallel: extending in the same direction
parasite: an organism that lives on or within a plant or animal of another species
    from which it obtains nutrients
parody: to imitate for purposes of satire
parable: a short, allegorical story designed to illustrate a moral lesson or religious
    principle
paragon: a model of excellence
paranoid: suffering from a baseless distrust of others

PAS/PAT/PATH: FEELING, SUFFERING, DISEASE

sympathy: harmony or agreement in feeling
empathy: the identification with the feelings or thoughts of others

compassion: a feeling of deep sympathy for someone struck by misfortune
accompanied by a desire to alleviate suffering

dispassionate: devoid of personal feeling or bias

impassive: showing or feeling no emotion

sociopath: a person whose behavior is antisocial and who lacks a sense of moral
responsibility

pathogenic: causing disease

PAU/PO/POV/PU: FEW, LITTLE, POOR

poverty: the condition of being poor

paucity: smallness of quantity; scarcity; scantiness

pauper: a person without any personal means of support

impoverish: to deplete

pusillanimous: lacking courage or resolution

puerile: childish, immature

PED: CHILD, EDUCATION

pedagogue: a teacher

pediatrician: a doctor who primarily has children as patients

pedant: one who displays learning ostentatiously

encyclopedia: book or set of books containing articles on various topics, covering
all branches of knowledge or of one particular subject

PED/POD: FOOT

pedal: a foot-operated lever or part used to control

pedestrian: a person who travels on foot

expedite: to speed up the progress of

impede: to retard progress by means of obstacles or hindrances

podium: a small platform for an orchestra conductor, speaker, etc.

antipodes: places diametrically opposite each other on the globe

PEN/PUN: TO PAY; TO COMPENSATE

penal: of or pertaining to punishment, as for crimes

penalty: a punishment imposed for a violation of law or rule

punitive: serving for, concerned with, or inflicting punishment

penance: a punishment undergone to express regret for a sin

penitent: contrite

PEND/PENS: TO HANG; TO WEIGHT; TO PAY

depend: to rely; to place trust in

stipend: a periodic payment; fixed or regular pay

compensate: to counterbalance, offset

indispensable: absolutely necessary, essential, or requisite

appendix: supplementary material at the end of a text

appendage: a limb or other subsidiary part that diverges from the central structure

PER: COMPLETELY

persistent: lasting or enduring tenaciously

perforate: to make a way through or into something

perplex: to cause to be puzzled or bewildered over what is not understood

peruse: to read with thoroughness or care

perfunctory: performed merely as routine duty

pertinacious: resolute

perspicacious: shrewd, astute

PERI: AROUND

perimeter: the border or outer boundary of a two-dimensional figure

periscope: an optical instrument for seeing objects in an obstructed field of vision

peripatetic: walking or traveling about; itinerant

PET/PIT: TO GO; TO SEEK; TO STRIVE

appetite: a desire for food or drink

compete: to strive to outdo another for acknowledgment

petition: a formally drawn request soliciting some benefit

centripetal: moving toward the center

impetuous: characterized by sudden or rash action or emotion

petulant: showing sudden irritation, esp. over some annoyance

PHIL: LOVE

philosophy: the rational investigation of the truths and principles of being, knowledge, or conduct

philatelist: one who loves or collects postage stamps

philology: the study of literary texts to establish their authenticity and determine their meaning

bibliophile: one who loves or collects books

PLAC: TO PLEASE

placid: pleasantly calm or peaceful

placebo: a substance with no pharmacological effect that eases symptoms in a patient who believes it to be a medicine

implacable: unable to be pleased

complacent: self-satisfied, unconcerned

complaisant: inclined or disposed to please

PLE: TO FILL

complete: having all parts or elements
deplete: to decrease seriously or exhaust the supply of
supplement: something added to supply a deficiency
implement: an instrument, tool, or utensil for accomplishing work
replete: abundantly supplied
plethora: excess, overabundance

PLEX/PLIC/PLY: TO FOLD, TWIST, TANGLE, OR BEND

complex: composed of many interconnected parts
replica: any close copy or reproduction
implicit: not expressly stated, implied
implicate: to show to be involved, usually in an incriminating manner
duplicity: deceitfulness in speech or conduct, double-dealing
supplicate: to make humble and earnest entreaty

PON/POS/POUND: TO PUT; TO PLACE

component: a constituent part, elemental ingredient
expose: to lay open to danger, attack, or harm
expound: to set forth in detail
juxtapose: to place close together or side by side, esp. for contract
repository: a receptacle or place where things are deposited

PORT: TO CARRY

import: to bring in from a foreign country
export: to transmit abroad
portable: easily carried
deportment: conduct, behavior
disport: to divert or amuse oneself
importune: to urge or press with excessive persistence

POST: AFTER

posthumous: after death
posterior: situated at the rear
posterity: succeeding in future generations collectively
post facto: after the fact

PRE: BEFORE

precarious: dependent on circumstances beyond one's control
precocious: unusually advanced or mature in mental development or talent
premonition: a feeling of anticipation over a future event

presentiment: foreboding
precedent: an act that serves as an example for subsequent situations
precept: a commandment given as a rule of action or conduct

PREHEND/PRISE: TO TAKE; TO GET; TO SEIZE

surprise: to strike with an unexpected feeling of wonder or astonishment
enterprise: a project undertaken
reprehensible: deserving rebuke or censure
comprise: to include or contain
reprisals: retaliation against an enemy
apprehend: to take into custody

PRO: MUCH, FOR, A LOT

prolific: highly fruitful
profuse: spending or giving freely
prodigal: wastefully or recklessly extravagant
prodigious: extraordinary in size, amount, or extent
proselytize: to convert or attempt to recruit
propound: to set forth for consideration
provident: having or showing foresight

PROB: TO PROVE; TO TEST

probe: to search or examine thoroughly
approbation: praise, consideration
opprobrium: the disgrace incurred by shameful conduct
reprobate: a depraved or wicked person
problematic: questionable
probity: honesty, high-mindedness

PUG: TO FIGHT

pugnacious: to quarrel or fight readily
impugn: to challenge as false
repugnant: objectionable or offensive
pugilist: a fighter or boxer

PUNC/PUNG/POIGN: TO POINT; TO PRICK

point: a sharp or tapering end
puncture: the act of piercing
pungent: caustic or sharply expressive
compunction: a feeling of uneasiness for doing wrong
punctilious: strict or exact in the observance of formalities
expunge: to erase, eliminate completely

QUE/QUIS: TO SEEK

acquire: to come into possession of
exquisite: of special beauty or charm
conquest: vanquishment
inquisitive: given to research, eager for knowledge
query: a question, inquiry
querulous: full of complaints
perquisite: a gratuity, tip

QUI: QUIET

quiet: making little or no sound
disquiet: lack of calm or peace
tranquil: free from commotion or tumult
acquiesce: to comply, give in
quiescence: the condition of being at rest, still, inactive

RID/RIS: TO LAUGH

riddle: a conundrum
derision: the act of mockery
risible: causing laughter

ROG: TO ASK

interrogate: to ask questions of, esp. formally
arrogant: making claims to superior importance or rights
abrogate: to abolish by formal means
surrogate: a person appointed to act for another
derogatory: belittling, disparaging
arrogate: to claim unwarrantably or presumptuously

SACR/SANCT/SECR: SACRED

sacred: devoted or dedicated to a deity or religious purpose
sacrifice: the offering of some living or inanimate thing to a deity in homage
sanctify: to make holy
sanction: authoritative permission or approval
execrable: abominable
sacrament: something regarded as possessing sacred character
sacrilege: the violation of anything sacred

SAL/SIL/SAULT/SULT: TO LEAP, TO JUMP

insult: to treat with contemptuous rudeness
assault: a sudden or violent attack

somersault: to roll the body end over end, making a complete revolution

salient: prominent or conspicuous

resilient: able to spring back to an original form after compression

insolent: boldly rude or disrespectful

exult: to show or feel triumphant joy

desultory: at random, unmethodical

SCI: TO KNOW

conscious: aware of one's own existence

conscience: the inner sense of what is right or wrong, impelling one toward right action

unconscionable: unscrupulous

omniscient: knowing everything

prescient: having knowledge of things before they happen

SCRIBE/SCRIP: TO WRITE

scribble: to write hastily or carelessly

describe: to tell or depict in words

script: handwriting

postscript: an addition or supplement

proscribe: to condemn as harmful or odious

ascribe: to credit or assign, as to a cause or course

conscription: draft

transcript: a written or typed copy

circumscribe: to draw a line around

SE: APART

select: to choose in preference to another

separate: to keep apart, divide

seduce: to lead astray

segregate: to separate or set apart from others

secede: to withdraw formally from an association

sequester: to remove or withdraw into solitude or retirement

sedition: incitement of discontent or rebellion against a government

SEC/SEQU: TO FOLLOW

second: next after the first

prosecute: to seek to enforce by legal process

sequence: the following of one thing after another

obsequious: fawning

non sequitur: an inference or a conclusion that does not follow from the premises

SED/SESS/SID: TO SIT; TO BE STILL; TO PLAN; TO PLOT

preside: to exercise management or control
resident: a person who lives in a place
sediment: the matter that settles to the bottom of a liquid
dissident: disagreeing, as in opinion or attitude
residual: remaining, leftover
subsidiary: serving to assist or supplement
insidious: intended to entrap or beguile
assiduous: diligent, persistent, hardworking

SENS/SENT: TO FEEL; TO BE AWARE

sense: any of the faculties by which humans and animals perceive stimuli
   originating outside the body
sensory: of or pertaining to the senses or sensation
sentiment: an attitude or feeling toward something
presentiment: a feeling that something is about to happen
dissent: to differ in opinion, esp. from the majority
resent: to feel or show displeasure
sentinel: a person or thing that stands watch
insensate: without feeling or sensitivity

SOL: TO LOOSEN; TO FREE

dissolve: to make a solution of, as by mixing in a liquid
soluble: capable of being dissolved or liquefied
resolution: a formal expression of opinion or intention made
dissolution: the act or process of dissolving into parts or elements
dissolute: indifferent to moral restraints
absolution: forgiveness for wrongdoing

SPEC/SPIC/SPIT: TO LOOK; TO SEE

perspective: one's mental view of facts, ideas, and their interrelationships
speculation: the contemplation or consideration of some subject
suspicious: inclined to suspect
spectrum: a broad range of related things that form a continuous series
retrospective: contemplative of past situations
circumspect: watchful and discreet, cautious
perspicacious: having keen mental perception and understanding
conspicuous: easily seen or noticed; readily observable
specious: deceptively attractive

STA/STI: TO STAND; TO BE IN PLACE

static: of bodies or forces at rest or in equilibrium

destitute: without means of subsistence

obstinate: stubbornly adhering to a purpose, opinion, or course of action

constitute: to make up

stasis: the state of equilibrium or inactivity caused by opposing equal forces

apostasy: renunciation of an object of one's previous loyalty

SUA: SMOOTH

suave: smoothly agreeable or polite

persuade: to encourage; to convince

dissuade: to deter

assuage: to make less severe, ease, relieve

SUB/SUP: BELOW

submissive: inclined or ready to submit

subsidiary: serving to assist or supplement

subliminal: existing or operating below the threshold of confidence

subtle: thin, tenuous, or rarefied

subterfuge: an artifice or expedient used to evade a rule

supposition: the act of assuming

SUPER/SUR: ABOVE

surpass: to go beyond in amount, extent, or degree

superlative: the highest kind or order

supersede: to replace in power, as by another person or thing

supercilious: arrogant, haughty, condescending

superfluous: extra, more than necessary

surmount: to get over or across, to prevail

surveillance: a watch kept over someone or something

TAC/TIC: TO BE SILENT

reticent: disposed to be silent or not to speak freely

tacit: unspoken understanding

taciturn: uncommunicative

TAIN/TEN/TENT/TIN: TO HOLD

detain: to keep from proceeding

pertain: to have reference or relation

tenacious: holding fast

abstention: the act of refraining voluntarily

tenure: the holding or possessing of anything
tenable: capable of being held, maintained, or defended
sustenance: nourishment, means of livelihood
pertinacious: persistent, stubborn

TEND/TENS/TENT/TENU: TO STRETCH; TO THIN

tension: the act of stretching or straining
tentative: of the nature of, or done as a trial, attempt
tendentious: having a predisposition towards a point of view
distend: to expand by stretching
attenuate: to weaken or reduce in force
extenuating: making less serious by offering excuses
contentious: quarrelsome, disagreeable, belligerent

THEO: GOD

atheist: one who does not believe in a deity or divine system
theocracy: a form of government in which a deity is recognized as the supreme ruler
theology: the study of divine things and the divine faith
apotheosis: glorification, glorified ideal

TRACT: TO DRAG; TO PULL; TO DRAW

tractor: a powerful vehicle used to pull farm machinery
attract: to draw either by physical force or by an appeal to emotions or senses
contract: a legally binding document
detract: to take away from, esp. a positive thing
abstract: to draw or pull away, remove
tractable: easily managed or controlled
protract: to prolong, draw out, extend

TRANS: ACROSS

transaction: the act of carrying on or conduct to a conclusion or settlement
transparent: easily seen through, recognized, or detected
transition: a change from one way of being to another
transgress: to violate a law, command, or moral code
transcendent: going beyond ordinary limits
intransigent: refusing to agree or compromise

US/UT: TO USE

abuse: to use wrongly or improperly
usage: a customary way of doing something
usurp: to seize and hold
utilitarian: efficient, functional, useful

VEN/VENT: TO COME OR TO MOVE TOWARD

convene: to assemble for some public purpose
venturesome: showing a disposition to undertake risks
intervene: to come between disputing factions, mediate
contravene: to come into conflict with
adventitious: accidental

VER: TRUTH

verdict: any judgment or decision
veracious: habitually truthful
verity: truthfulness
verisimilitude: the appearance or semblance of truth
aver: to affirm, to declare to be true

VERD: GREEN

verdant: green with vegetation; inexperienced
verdure: fresh, rich vegetation

VERS/VERT: TO TURN

controversy: a public dispute involving a matter of opinion
revert: to return to a former habit
diverse: of a different kind, form, character
aversion: dislike
introvert: a person concerned primarily with inner thoughts and feelings
extrovert: an outgoing person
inadvertent: unintentional
covert: hidden, clandestine
avert: to turn away from

VI: LIFE

vivid: strikingly bright or intense
vicarious: performed, exercised, received, or suffered in place of another
viable: capable of living
vivacity: the quality of being lively, animated, spirited
joie de vivre: joy of life (French expression)
convivial: sociable

VID/VIS: TO SEE

evident: plain or clear to the sight or understanding
video: the elements of television pertaining to the transmission or reception
   of the image

adviser: one who gives counsel
survey: to view in a general or comprehensive way
vista: a view or prospect

VIL: BASE, MEAN

vilify: to slander, to defame
revile: to criticize with harsh language
vile: loathsome, unpleasant

VOC/VOK: TO CALL

vocabulary: the stock of words used by or known to a particular person or group
advocate: to support or urge by argument
equivocate: to use ambiguous or unclear expressions
vocation: a particular occupation
avocation: something one does in addition to a principle occupation
vociferous: crying out noisily
convoke: to call together
invoke: to call on a deity

VOL: TO WISH

voluntary: undertaken of one's own accord or by free choice
malevolent: characterized by or expressing bad will
benevolent: characterized by or expressing goodwill
volition: free choice, free will; act of choosing

VOR: TO EAT

voracious: having a great appetite
carnivorous: meat-eating
omnivorous: eating or absorbing everything

TOP GRE WORDS IN CONTEXT

The GRE tests the same kinds of words over and over again. Here you will find the most popular GRE words with their definitions in context to help you to remember them. If you see a word that's unfamiliar to you, take a moment to study the definition and, most importantly, reread the sentence with the word's definition in mind.

Remember: Learning vocabulary words in context is one of the best ways for your brain to retain the words' meanings. A broader vocabulary will serve you well on all four GRE Verbal question types and will also be extremely helpful in the Analytical Writing section.

ABATE: TO REDUCE IN AMOUNT, DEGREE, OR SEVERITY

As the hurricane's force ABATED, the winds dropped and the sea became calm.

ABSCOND: TO LEAVE SECRETLY

The patron ABSCONDED from the restaurant without paying his bill by sneaking out the back door.

ABSTAIN: TO CHOOSE NOT TO DO SOMETHING:

She ABSTAINED from choosing a mouthwatering dessert from the tray.

ABYSS: AN EXTREMELY DEEP HOLE

The submarine dove into the ABYSS to chart the previously unseen depths.

ADULTERATE: TO MAKE IMPURE

The restaurateur made his ketchup last longer by ADULTERATING it with water.

ADVOCATE: TO SPEAK IN FAVOR OF

The vegetarian ADVOCATED a diet containing no meat.

AESTHETIC: CONCERNING THE APPRECIATION OF BEAUTY

Followers of the AESTHETIC Movement regarded the pursuit of beauty as the only true purpose of art.

AGGRANDIZE: TO INCREASE IN POWER, INFLUENCE, AND REPUTATION

The supervisor sought to AGGRANDIZE himself by claiming that the achievements of his staff were actually his own.

ALLEVIATE: TO MAKE MORE BEARABLE

Taking aspirin helps to ALLEVIATE a headache.

AMALGAMATE: TO COMBINE; TO MIX TOGETHER

Giant Industries AMALGAMATED with Mega Products to form Giant-Mega Products Incorporated.

AMBIGUOUS: DOUBTFUL OR UNCERTAIN; ABLE TO BE INTERPRETED SEVERAL WAYS

The directions she gave were so AMBIGUOUS that we disagreed on which way to turn.

AMELIORATE: TO MAKE BETTER; TO IMPROVE

The doctor was able to AMELIORATE the patient's suffering using painkillers.

ANACHRONISM: SOMETHING OUT OF PLACE IN TIME

The aged hippie used ANACHRONISTIC phrases like *groovy* and *far out* that had not been popular for years.

ANALOGOUS: SIMILAR OR ALIKE IN SOME WAY; EQUIVALENT TO

In a famous argument for the existence of God, the universe is ANALOGOUS to a mechanical timepiece, the creation of a divinely intelligent "clockmaker."

ANOMALY: DEVIATION FROM WHAT IS NORMAL

Albino animals may display too great an ANOMALY in their coloring to attract normally colored mates.

ANTAGONIZE: TO ANNOY OR PROVOKE TO ANGER

The child discovered that he could ANTAGONIZE the cat by pulling its tail.

ANTIPATHY: EXTREME DISLIKE

The ANTIPATHY between the French and the English regularly erupted into open warfare.

APATHY: LACK OF INTEREST OR EMOTION

The APATHY of voters is so great that less than half the people who are eligible to vote actually bother to do so.

ARBITRATE: TO JUDGE A DISPUTE BETWEEN TWO OPPOSING PARTIES

Since the couple could not come to agreement, a judge was forced to ARBITRATE their divorce proceedings.

ARCHAIC: ANCIENT, OLD-FASHIONED

Her ARCHAIC Commodore computer could not run the latest software.

ARDOR: INTENSE AND PASSIONATE FEELING

Bishop's ARDOR for landscape was evident when he passionately described the beauty of the scenic Hudson Valley.

ARTICULATE: ABLE TO SPEAK CLEARLY AND EXPRESSIVELY

She is such an ARTICULATE defender of labor that unions are among her strongest supporters.

ASSUAGE: TO MAKE SOMETHING UNPLEASANT LESS SEVERE

Serena used aspirin to ASSUAGE her pounding headache.

ATTENUATE: TO REDUCE IN FORCE OR DEGREE; TO WEAKEN

The Bill of Rights ATTENUATED the traditional power of government to change laws at will.

AUDACIOUS: FEARLESS AND DARING

Her AUDACIOUS nature allowed her to fulfill her dream of skydiving.

AUSTERE: SEVERE OR STERN IN APPEARANCE; UNDECORATED

The lack of decoration makes Zen temples seem AUSTERE to the untrained eye.

BANAL: PREDICTABLE, CLICHÉD, BORING

He used BANAL phrases like *Have a nice day*, or *Another day, another dollar.*

BOLSTER: TO SUPPORT; TO PROP UP

The presence of giant footprints BOLSTERED the argument that Sasquatch was in the area.

BOMBASTIC: POMPOUS IN SPEECH AND MANNER

The dictator's speeches were mostly BOMBASTIC; his boasting and outrageous claims had no basis in fact.

CACOPHONY: HARSH, JARRING NOISE

The junior high orchestra created an almost unbearable CACOPHONY as they tried to tune their instruments.

CANDID: IMPARTIAL AND HONEST IN SPEECH

The observations of a child can be charming since they are CANDID and unpretentious.

CAPRICIOUS: CHANGING ONE'S MIND QUICKLY AND OFTEN

Queen Elizabeth I was quite CAPRICIOUS; her courtiers could never be sure which of their number would catch her fancy.

CASTIGATE: TO PUNISH OR CRITICIZE HARSHLY

Americans are amazed at how harshly the authorities in Singapore CASTIGATE perpetrators of what would be considered minor crimes in the United States.

CATALYST: SOMETHING THAT BRINGS ABOUT A CHANGE IN SOMETHING ELSE

The imposition of harsh taxes was the CATALYST that finally brought on the revolution.

CAUSTIC: BITING IN WIT

Dorothy Parker gained her reputation for CAUSTIC wit from her cutting, yet clever, insults.

CHAOS: GREAT DISORDER OR CONFUSION

In most religious traditions, God created an ordered universe from CHAOS.

CHAUVINIST: SOMEONE PREJUDICED IN FAVOR OF A GROUP TO WHICH HE OR SHE BELONGS

The attitude that men are inherently superior to women and therefore must be obeyed is common among male CHAUVINISTS.

CHICANERY: DECEPTION BY MEANS OF CRAFT OR GUILE

Dishonest used car salespeople often use CHICANERY to sell their beat-up old cars.

COGENT: CONVINCING AND WELL REASONED

Swayed by the COGENT argument of the defense, the jury had no choice but to acquit the defendant.

CONDONE: TO OVERLOOK, PARDON, OR DISREGARD

Some theorists believe that failing to prosecute minor crimes is the same as CONDONING an air of lawlessness.

CONVOLUTED: INTRICATE AND COMPLICATED

Although many people bought *A Brief History of Time*, few could follow its CONVOLUTED ideas and theories.

CORROBORATE: TO PROVIDE SUPPORTING EVIDENCE

Fingerprints CORROBORATED the witness's testimony that he saw the defendant in the victim's apartment.

CREDULOUS: TOO TRUSTING; GULLIBLE

Although some four-year-olds believe in the Easter Bunny, only the most CREDULOUS nine-year-olds believe in him.

CRESCENDO: STEADILY INCREASING VOLUME OR FORCE

The CRESCENDO of tension became unbearable as Evel Knievel prepared to jump his motorcycle over the school buses.

DECORUM: APPROPRIATENESS OF BEHAVIOR OR CONDUCT; PROPRIETY

The countess complained that the vulgar peasants lacked the DECORUM appropriate for a visit to the palace.

DEFERENCE: RESPECT, COURTESY

The respectful young law clerk treated the Supreme Court justice with the utmost DEFERENCE.

DERIDE: TO SPEAK OF OR TREAT WITH CONTEMPT; TO MOCK

The awkward child was often DERIDED by his "cooler" peers.

DESICCATE: TO DRY OUT THOROUGHLY

After a few weeks of lying on the desert's baking sands, the cow's carcass became completely DESICCATED.

DESULTORY: JUMPING FROM ONE THING TO ANOTHER; DISCONNECTED

Diane had a DESULTORY academic record; she had changed majors 12 times in three years.

DIATRIBE: AN ABUSIVE, CONDEMNATORY SPEECH

The trucker bellowed a DIATRIBE at the driver who had cut him off.

DIFFIDENT: LACKING SELF-CONFIDENCE

Steve's DIFFIDENT manner during the job interview stemmed from his nervous nature and lack of experience in the field.

DILATE: TO MAKE LARGER; TO EXPAND

When you enter a darkened room, the pupils of your eyes DILATE to let in more light.

DILATORY: INTENDED TO DELAY

The congressman used DILATORY measures to delay the passage of the bill.

DILETTANTE: SOMEONE WITH AN AMATEURISH AND SUPERFICIAL INTEREST IN A TOPIC

Jerry's friends were such DILETTANTES that they seemed to have new jobs and hobbies every week.

DIRGE: A FUNERAL HYMN OR MOURNFUL SPEECH

Melville wrote the poem "A DIRGE for James McPherson" for the funeral of a Union general who was killed in 1864.

DISABUSE: TO SET RIGHT; TO FREE FROM ERROR

Galileo's observations DISABUSED scholars of the notion that the sun revolved around the earth.

DISCERN: TO PERCEIVE; TO RECOGNIZE

It is easy to DISCERN the difference between butter and butter-flavored topping.

DISPARATE: FUNDAMENTALLY DIFFERENT; ENTIRELY UNLIKE

Although the twins appear to be identical physically, their personalities are DISPARATE.

DISSEMBLE: TO PRESENT A FALSE APPEARANCE; TO DISGUISE ONE'S REAL INTENTIONS OR CHARACTER

The villain could DISSEMBLE to the police no longer—he admitted the deed and tore up the floor to reveal the body of the old man.

DISSONANCE: A HARSH AND DISAGREEABLE COMBINATION, OFTEN OF SOUNDS

Cognitive DISSONANCE is the inner conflict produced when long-standing beliefs are contradicted by new evidence.

DOGMA: A FIRMLY HELD OPINION, OFTEN A RELIGIOUS BELIEF

Linus's central DOGMA was that children who believed in the Great Pumpkin would be rewarded.

DOGMATIC: DICTATORIAL IN ONE'S OPINIONS

The dictator was DOGMATIC—he, and only he, was right.

DUPE: TO DECEIVE (V.); A PERSON WHO IS EASILY DECEIVED (N.)

Bugs Bunny was able to DUPE Elmer Fudd by dressing up as a lady rabbit.

ECLECTIC: SELECTING FROM OR MADE UP FROM A VARIETY OF SOURCES

Budapest's architecture is an ECLECTIC mix of Eastern and Western styles.

EFFICACY: EFFECTIVENESS

The EFFICACY of penicillin was unsurpassed when it was first introduced; the drug completely eliminated almost all bacterial infections for which it was administered.

ELEGY: A SORROWFUL POEM OR SPEECH

Although Thomas Gray's "ELEGY Written in a Country Churchyard" is about death and loss, it urges its readers to endure this life and to trust in spirituality.

ELOQUENT: PERSUASIVE AND MOVING, ESPECIALLY IN SPEECH

The Gettysburg Address is moving not only because of its lofty sentiments but also because of its ELOQUENT words.

EMULATE: TO COPY; TO TRY TO EQUAL OR EXCEL

The graduate student sought to EMULATE his professor in every way, copying not only how she taught but also how she conducted herself outside of class.

ENERVATE: TO REDUCE IN STRENGTH

The guerrillas hoped that a series of surprise attacks would ENERVATE the regular army.

ENGENDER: TO PRODUCE, CAUSE, OR BRING ABOUT

His fear and hatred of clowns was ENGENDERED when he witnessed the death of his father at the hands of a clown.

ENIGMA: A PUZZLE; A MYSTERY

Speaking in riddles and dressed in old robes, the artist gained a reputation as something of an ENIGMA.

ENUMERATE: TO COUNT, LIST, OR ITEMIZE

Moses returned from the mountain with tablets on which the commandments were ENUMERATED.

EPHEMERAL: LASTING A SHORT TIME

The lives of mayflies seem EPHEMERAL to us, since the flies' average life span is a matter of hours.

EQUIVOCATE: TO USE EXPRESSIONS OF DOUBLE MEANING IN ORDER TO MISLEAD

When faced with criticism of his policies, the politician EQUIVOCATED and left all parties thinking he agreed with them.

ERRATIC: WANDERING AND UNPREDICTABLE

The plot seemed predictable until it suddenly took a series of ERRATIC turns that surprised the audience.

ERUDITE: LEARNED, SCHOLARLY, BOOKISH

The annual meeting of philosophy professors was a gathering of the most ERUDITE, well-published individuals in the field.

ESOTERIC: KNOWN OR UNDERSTOOD BY ONLY A FEW

Only a handful of experts are knowledgeable about the ESOTERIC world of particle physics.

ESTIMABLE: ADMIRABLE

Most people consider it ESTIMABLE that Mother Teresa spent her life helping the poor of India.

EULOGY: SPEECH IN PRAISE OF SOMEONE

His best friend gave the EULOGY, outlining his many achievements and talents.

EUPHEMISM: USE OF AN INOFFENSIVE WORD OR PHRASE IN PLACE OF A MORE DISTASTEFUL ONE

The funeral director preferred to use the EUPHEMISM *sleeping* instead of the word *dead.*

EXACERBATE: TO MAKE WORSE

It is unwise to take aspirin to try to relieve heartburn; instead of providing relief, the drug will only EXACERBATE the problem.

EXCULPATE: TO CLEAR FROM BLAME; PROVE INNOCENT

The adversarial legal system is intended to convict those who are guilty and to EXCULPATE those who are innocent.

EXIGENT: URGENT; REQUIRING IMMEDIATE ACTION

The patient was losing blood so rapidly that it was EXIGENT to stop the source of the bleeding.

EXONERATE: TO CLEAR OF BLAME

The fugitive was EXONERATED when another criminal confessed to committing the crime.

EXPLICIT: CLEARLY STATED OR SHOWN; FORTHRIGHT IN EXPRESSION

The owners of the house left a list of EXPLICIT instructions detailing their house-sitters' duties, including a schedule for watering the house plants.

FANATICAL: ACTING EXCESSIVELY ENTHUSIASTIC; FILLED WITH EXTREME, UNQUESTIONED DEVOTION

The stormtroopers were FANATICAL in their devotion to the Emperor, readily sacrificing their lives for him.

FAWN: TO GROVEL

The understudy FAWNED over the director in hopes of being cast in the part on a permanent basis.

FERVID: INTENSELY EMOTIONAL; FEVERISH

The fans of Maria Callas were unusually FERVID, doing anything to catch a glimpse of the great opera singer.

FLORID: EXCESSIVELY DECORATED OR EMBELLISHED

The palace had been decorated in an excessively FLORID style; every surface had been carved and gilded.

FOMENT: TO AROUSE OR INCITE

The protesters tried to FOMENT feeling against the war through their speeches and demonstrations.

FRUGALITY: A TENDENCY TO BE THRIFTY OR CHEAP

Scrooge McDuck's FRUGALITY was so great that he accumulated enough wealth to fill a giant storehouse with money.

GARRULOUS: TENDING TO TALK A LOT

The GARRULOUS parakeet distracted its owner with its continuous talking.

GREGARIOUS: OUTGOING, SOCIABLE

She was so GREGARIOUS that when she found herself alone, she felt quite sad.

GUILE: DECEIT OR TRICKERY

Since he was not fast enough to catch the roadrunner on foot, the coyote resorted to GUILE in an effort to trap his enemy.

GULLIBLE: EASILY DECEIVED

The con man pretended to be a bank officer so as to fool GULLIBLE bank customers into giving him their account information.

HOMOGENOUS: OF A SIMILAR KIND

The class was fairly HOMOGENOUS, since almost all of the students were senior journalism majors.

ICONOCLAST: ONE WHO OPPOSES ESTABLISHED BELIEFS, CUSTOMS, AND INSTITUTIONS

His lack of regard for traditional beliefs soon established him as an ICONOCLAST.

IMPERTURBABLE: NOT CAPABLE OF BEING DISTURBED

The counselor had so much experience dealing with distraught children that she seemed IMPERTURBABLE, even when faced with the wildest tantrums.

IMPERVIOUS: IMPOSSIBLE TO PENETRATE; INCAPABLE OF BEING AFFECTED

A good raincoat will be IMPERVIOUS to moisture.

IMPETUOUS: QUICK TO ACT WITHOUT THINKING

It is not good for an investment broker to be IMPETUOUS, since much thought should be given to all the possible options.

IMPLACABLE: UNABLE TO BE CALMED DOWN OR MADE PEACEFUL

His rage at the betrayal was so great that he remained IMPLACABLE for weeks.

INCHOATE: NOT FULLY FORMED; DISORGANIZED

The ideas expressed in Nietzsche's mature work also appear in an INCHOATE form in his earliest writing.

INGENUOUS: SHOWING INNOCENCE OR CHILDLIKE SIMPLICITY

She was so INGENUOUS that her friends feared that her innocence and trustfulness would be exploited when she visited the big city.

INIMICAL: HOSTILE, UNFRIENDLY

Even though the children had grown up together, they were INIMICAL to each other at school.

INNOCUOUS: HARMLESS

Some snakes are poisonous, but most species are INNOCUOUS and pose no danger to humans.

INSIPID: LACKING INTEREST OR FLAVOR

The critic claimed that the painting was INSIPID, containing no interesting qualities at all.

INTRANSIGENT: UNCOMPROMISING; REFUSING TO BE RECONCILED

The professor was INTRANSIGENT on the deadline, insisting that everyone turn the assignment in at the same time.

INUNDATE: TO OVERWHELM; TO COVER WITH WATER

The tidal wave INUNDATED Atlantis, which was lost beneath the water.

IRASCIBLE: EASILY MADE ANGRY

Attila the Hun's IRASCIBLE and violent nature made all who dealt with him fear for their lives.

LACONIC: USING FEW WORDS

She was a LACONIC poet who built her reputation on using words as sparingly
as possible.

LAMENT: TO EXPRESS SORROW; TO GRIEVE

The children continued to LAMENT the death of the goldfish weeks after its demise.

LAUD: TO GIVE PRAISE; TO GLORIFY

Parades and fireworks were staged to LAUD the success of the rebels.

LAVISH: TO GIVE UNSPARINGLY (V.); EXTREMELY GENEROUS OR EXTRAVAGANT (ADJ.)

She LAVISHED the puppy with so many treats that it soon became overweight
and spoiled.

LETHARGIC: ACTING IN AN INDIFFERENT OR SLOW, SLUGGISH MANNER

The clerk was so LETHARGIC that, even when the store was slow, he always had a
long line in front of him.

LOQUACIOUS: TALKATIVE

She was naturally LOQUACIOUS, which was a problem in situations in which
listening was more important than talking.

LUCID: CLEAR AND EASILY UNDERSTOOD

The explanations were written in a simple and LUCID manner so that students
were immediately able to apply what they learned.

LUMINOUS: BRIGHT, BRILLIANT, GLOWING

The park was bathed in LUMINOUS sunshine, which warmed the bodies and the
souls of the visitors.

MALINGER: TO EVADE RESPONSIBILITY BY PRETENDING TO BE ILL

A common way to avoid the draft was by MALINGERING—pretending to be mentally
or physically ill so as to avoid being taken by the Army.

MALLEABLE: CAPABLE OF BEING SHAPED

Gold is the most MALLEABLE of precious metals; it can easily be formed into
almost any shape.

METAPHOR: A FIGURE OF SPEECH COMPARING TWO DIFFERENT THINGS; A SYMBOL

The METAPHOR "a sea of troubles" suggests a lot of troubles by comparing their
number to the vastness of the sea.

METICULOUS: EXTREMELY CAREFUL ABOUT DETAILS

To find all the clues at the crime scene, the investigators METICULOUSLY examined every inch of the area.

MISANTHROPE: A PERSON WHO DISLIKES OTHERS

The character Scrooge in *A Christmas Carol* is such a MISANTHROPE that even the sight of children singing makes him angry.

MITIGATE: TO SOFTEN; TO LESSEN

A judge may MITIGATE a sentence if she decides that a person committed a crime out of need.

MOLLIFY: TO CALM OR MAKE LESS SEVERE

Their argument was so intense that is was difficult to believe any compromise would MOLLIFY them.

MONOTONY: LACK OF VARIATION

The MONOTONY of the sound of the dripping faucet almost drove the research assistant crazy.

NAIVE: LACKING SOPHISTICATION OR EXPERIENCE

Having never traveled before, the hillbillies were more NAIVE than the people they met in Beverly Hills.

OBDURATE: HARDENED IN FEELING; RESISTANT TO PERSUASION

The president was completely OBDURATE on the issue, and no amount of persuasion would change his mind.

OBSEQUIOUS: OVERLY SUBMISSIVE AND EAGER TO PLEASE

The OBSEQUIOUS new associate made sure to compliment her supervisor's tie and agree with him on every issue.

OBSTINATE: STUBBORN, UNYIELDING

The OBSTINATE child could not be made to eat any food that he disliked.

OBVIATE: TO PREVENT; TO MAKE UNNECESSARY

The river was shallow enough to wade across at many points, which OBVIATED the need for a bridge.

OCCLUDE: TO STOP UP; TO PREVENT THE PASSAGE OF

A shadow is thrown across the earth's surface during a solar eclipse, when the light from the sun is OCCLUDED by the moon.

ONEROUS: TROUBLESOME AND OPPRESSIVE; BURDENSOME

The assignment was so extensive and difficult to manage that it proved ONEROUS to the team in charge of it.

OPAQUE: IMPOSSIBLE TO SEE THROUGH; PREVENTING THE PASSAGE OF LIGHT

The heavy buildup of dirt and grime on the windows made them almost OPAQUE.

OPPROBRIUM: PUBLIC DISGRACE

After the scheme to embezzle the elderly was made public, the treasurer resigned in utter OPPROBRIUM.

OSTENTATION: EXCESSIVE SHOWINESS

The OSTENTATION of the Sun King's court is evident in the lavish decoration and luxuriousness of his palace at Versailles.

PARADOX: A CONTRADICTION OR DILEMMA

It is a PARADOX that those most in need of medical attention are often those least able to obtain it.

PARAGON: MODEL OF EXCELLENCE OR PERFECTION

She is the PARAGON of what a judge should be: honest, intelligent, hardworking, and just.

PEDANT: SOMEONE WHO SHOWS OFF LEARNING

The graduate instructor's tedious and excessive commentary on the subject soon gained her a reputation as a PEDANT.

PERFIDIOUS: WILLING TO BETRAY ONE'S TRUST

The actress' PERFIDIOUS companion revealed all of her intimate secrets to the gossip columnist.

PERFUNCTORY: DONE IN A ROUTINE WAY; INDIFFERENT

The machinelike bank teller processed the transaction and gave the waiting customer a PERFUNCTORY smile.

PERMEATE: TO PENETRATE

This miraculous new cleaning fluid is able to PERMEATE stains and dissolve them in minutes!

PHILANTHROPY: CHARITY; A DESIRE OR EFFORT TO PROMOTE GOODNESS

New York's Metropolitan Museum of Art owes much of its collection to the PHILANTHROPY of private collectors who willed their estates to the museum.

PLACATE: TO SOOTHE OR PACIFY

The burglar tried to PLACATE the snarling dog by saying, "Nice doggy," and offering it a treat.

PLASTIC: ABLE TO BE MOLDED, ALTERED, OR BENT

The new material was very PLASTIC and could be formed into products of vastly different shape.

PLETHORA: EXCESS

Assuming that more was better, the defendant offered the judge a PLETHORA of excuses.

PRAGMATIC: PRACTICAL AS OPPOSED TO IDEALISTIC

While daydreaming gamblers think they can get rich by frequenting casinos, PRAGMATIC gamblers realize that the odds are heavily stacked against them.

PRECIPITATE: TO THROW VIOLENTLY OR BRING ABOUT ABRUPTLY; LACKING DELIBERATION

Upon learning that the couple married after knowing each other only two months, friends and family members expected such a PRECIPITATE marriage to end in divorce.

PREVARICATE: TO LIE OR DEVIATE FROM THE TRUTH

Rather than admit that he had overslept again, the employee PREVARICATED and claimed that heavy traffic had prevented him from arriving at work on time.

PRISTINE: FRESH AND CLEAN; UNCORRUPTED

Since concerted measures had been taken to prevent looting, the archeological site was still PRISTINE when researchers arrived.

PRODIGAL: LAVISH, WASTEFUL

The PRODIGAL son quickly wasted all of his inheritance on a lavish lifestyle devoted to pleasure.

PROLIFERATE: TO INCREASE IN NUMBER QUICKLY

Although he only kept two guinea pigs initially, they PROLIFERATED to such an extent that he soon had dozens.

PROPITIATE: TO CONCILIATE; TO APPEASE

The management PROPITIATED the irate union by agreeing to raise wages for its members.

PROPRIETY: CORRECT BEHAVIOR; OBEDIENCE TO RULES AND CUSTOMS

The aristocracy maintained a high level of PROPRIETY, adhering to even the most minor social rules.

PRUDENCE: WISDOM, CAUTION, OR RESTRAINT

The college student exhibited PRUDENCE by obtaining practical experience along with her studies, which greatly strengthened her résumé.

PUNGENT: SHARP AND IRRITATING TO THE SENSES

The smoke from the burning tires was extremely PUNGENT.

QUIESCENT: MOTIONLESS

Many animals are QUIESCENT over the winter months, minimizing activity in order to conserve energy.

RAREFY: TO MAKE THINNER OR SPARSER

Since the atmosphere RAREFIES as altitudes increase, the air at the top of very tall mountains is too thin to breathe.

REPUDIATE: TO REJECT THE VALIDITY OF

The old woman's claim that she was Russian royalty was REPUDIATED when DNA tests showed she was not related to them.

RETICENT: SILENT, RESERVED

Physically small and RETICENT in her speech, Joan Didion often went unnoticed by those upon whom she was reporting.

RHETORIC: EFFECTIVE WRITING OR SPEAKING

Lincoln's talent for RHETORIC was evident in his beautifully expressed Gettysburg Address.

SATIATE: TO SATISFY FULLY OR OVERINDULGE

His desire for power was so great that nothing less than complete control of the country could SATIATE it.

SOPORIFIC: CAUSING SLEEP OR LETHARGY

The movie proved to be so SOPORIFIC that soon loud snores were heard throughout the theater.

SPECIOUS: DECEPTIVELY ATTRACTIVE; SEEMINGLY PLAUSIBLE BUT FALLACIOUS

The student's SPECIOUS excuse for being late sounded legitimate but was proved otherwise when her teacher called her home.

STIGMA: A MARK OF SHAME OR DISCREDIT

In *The Scarlet Letter*, Hester Prynne was required to wear the letter *A* on her clothes as a public STIGMA for her adultery.

STOLID: UNEMOTIONAL; LACKING SENSITIVITY

The prisoner appeared STOLID and unaffected by the judge's harsh sentence.

SUBLIME: LOFTY OR GRAND

The music was so SUBLIME that it transformed the rude surroundings into a special place.

TACIT: DONE WITHOUT USING WORDS

Although not a word had been said, everyone in the room knew that a TACIT agreement had been made about which course of action to take.

TACITURN: SILENT, NOT TALKATIVE

The clerk's TACITURN nature earned him the nickname "Silent Bob."

TIRADE: LONG, HARSH SPEECH OR VERBAL ATTACK

Observers were shocked at the manager's TIRADE over such a minor mistake.

TORPOR: EXTREME MENTAL AND PHYSICAL SLUGGISHNESS

After surgery, the patient experienced TORPOR until the anesthesia wore off.

TRANSITORY: TEMPORARY, LASTING A BRIEF TIME

The reporter lived a TRANSITORY life, staying in one place only long enough to cover the current story.

VACILLATE: TO SWAY PHYSICALLY; TO BE INDECISIVE

The customer held up the line as he VACILLATED between ordering chocolate chip or rocky road ice cream.

VENERATE: TO RESPECT DEEPLY

In a traditional Confucian society, the young VENERATE their elders, deferring to the elders' wisdom and experience.

VERACITY: FILLED WITH TRUTH AND ACCURACY

She had a reputation for VERACITY, so everyone trusted her description of events.

VERBOSE: WORDY

The professor's answer was so VERBOSE that his student forgot what the original question had been.

VEX: TO ANNOY

The old man who loved his peace and quiet, was VEXED by his neighbor's loud music.

VOLATILE: EASILY AROUSED OR CHANGEABLE; LIVELY OR EXPLOSIVE

His VOLATILE personality made it difficult to predict his reaction to anything.

WAVER: TO FLUCTUATE BETWEEN CHOICES

If you WAVER too long before making a decision about which testing site to register for, you may not get your first choice.

WHIMSICAL: ACTING IN A FANCIFUL OR CAPRICIOUS MANNER; UNPREDICTABLE

The ballet was WHIMSICAL, delighting the children with its imaginative characters and unpredictable sets.

ZEAL: PASSION, EXCITEMENT

She brought her typical ZEAL to the project, sparking enthusiasm in the other team members.

COMMONLY CONFUSED WORDS

Already—by this or that time, previously
He already completed his work.

All ready—completely prepared
The students were all ready to take their exam.

Altogether—entirely, completely
I am altogether certain that I turned in my homework.

All together—in the same place
She kept the figurines all together on her mantle.

Capital—a city containing the seat of government; the wealth or funds owned by a business or individual, resources
Atlanta is the capital of Georgia.
The company's capital gains have diminished in recent years.

Capitol—the building in which a legislative body meets.
Our trip included a visit to the Capitol building in Washington, D.C.

Coarse—rough, not smooth; lacking refinement
The truck's large wheels enabled it to navigate the coarse, rough terrain.
His coarse language prevented him from getting hired for the job.

Course—path; series of classes or studies
James's favorite course is biology.
The doctor suggested that Amy rest and let the disease run its course.

Here—in this location
George Washington used to live here.

Hear—to listen to or to perceive by the ear
Did you hear the question?

Its—a personal pronoun that shows possession
Please put the book back in its place.

It's—the contraction of *it is*
It's snowing outside.

Lead—to act as a leader, to go first, or to take a superior position
The guide will lead us through the forest.

Led—past tense of lead
The guide led us through the forest.

Lead—a metal
It is dangerous to inhale fumes from paint containing lead.

Loose—free, to set free, not tight
She always wears loose clothing when she does yoga.

Lose—to become without
Use a bookmark so you don't lose your place in your book.

Passed—the past tense of *pass*
We passed by her house on Sunday.

Past—that which has gone by or elapsed in time
In the past, Abby never used to study.
We drove past her house.

Principal—the head of a school; main or important

The quarterback's injury is the principal reason the team lost.

The principal of the school meets with parents regularly.

Principle—a law, doctrine, or rule

A just society is based on principles of fairness.

Stationary—fixed, not moving

Thomas rode a stationary bicycle at the gym.

Stationery—paper used for letter writing

The principal's stationery has the school's logo on the top.

Their—possessive of *they*

Pau and Ben studied for their test together.

There—a place; in that matter or respect

There are several question types on the GRE.

Please hang up your jacket over there.

They're—contraction of *they are*

Be careful of the bushes as they're filled with thorns.

MATH REFERENCE

The math on the GRE covers a lot of ground—from basic algebra to symbol problems to geometry. Don't let yourself be intimidated.

We've highlighted the 100 most important concepts that you need to know and divided them into three levels. The GRE Quantitative section tests your understanding of a relatively limited number of mathematical concepts, all of which you will be able to learn.

Level 1 is the most basic. You can't answer any GRE math questions if you don't know Level 1 math. Most people preparing to take the GRE are already pretty good at Level 1 math, but look over the Level 1 list just to make sure you're comfortable with he basics.

Level 2 is where most people start their review of math. Level 2 skills and formulas come into play quite frequently on the GRE, especially in the medium and hard questions.

Level 3 is the hardest math you'll find on the GRE. Don't spend a lot of time on Level 3 if you still have gaps in Level 2, but once you've mastered Level 2, tackling Level 3 can put you over the top.

LEVEL 1 (Math You Probably Already Know)

1. How to add, subtract, multiply, and divide WHOLE NUMBERS

2. How to add, subtract, multiply, and divide FRACTIONS

3. How to add, subtract, multiply, and divide DECIMALS

4. How to convert FRACTIONS TO DECIMALS and DECIMALS TO FRACTIONS

5. How to add, subtract, multiply, and divide POSITIVE AND NEGATIVE NUMBERS

6. How to plot points on the NUMBER LINE

7. How to plug a number into an ALGEBRAIC EXPRESSION

8. How to SOLVE a simple EQUATION

9. How to add and subtract LINE SEGMENTS

10. How to find the THIRD ANGLE of a TRIANGLE, given the other two angles

LEVEL 2 (Math You Might Need to Review)

11. **How to use PEMDAS**

When you're given an ugly arithmetic expression, it's important to know the order of operations. Just remember PEMDAS (as in "Please excuse my dear Aunt Sally"). What PEMDAS means is this: Clean up **Parentheses** first; then deal with **Exponents**; then do the **Multiplication** and **Division** together, going from left to right; and finally do the **Addition** and **Subtraction** together, again going from left to right.

Example: $9 - 2 \times (5 - 3)^2 + 6 \div 3 =$

Begin with the parentheses:
$$9 - 2 \times (2)^2 + 6 \div 3 =$$

Then do the exponent:
$$9 - 2 \times 4 + 6 \div 3 =$$

Now do multiplication and division from left to right:
$$9 - 8 + 2 =$$

Finally, do addition and subtraction from left to right:
$$9 - 8 + 2 = 1 + 2 = 3$$

12. **How to use the PERCENT FORMULA**

Identify the part, the percent, and the whole.

$$Part = \frac{percent}{100} \times whole$$

Find the part.

Example: What is 12 percent of 25?

Setup: $Part = \dfrac{12}{100} \times 25 = 3$

Find the percent.

Example: 45 is what percent of 9?

$$\frac{45}{9} = \frac{\%}{100} \times 9 / 9$$

$$100 \times 5 = \frac{\%}{100} \times 100$$

$$500 = \%$$

Setup: $45 = \text{Percent} \times 9$

$$\text{Percent} = \frac{45}{9} = 5 = 5 \times 100\% = 500\%$$

Find the whole.

Example: 15 is $\frac{3}{5}$ percent of what number?

Setup: $15 = \frac{3}{5}\left(\frac{1}{100}\right) \times \text{whole}$

$$15 = \frac{3}{500} \times \text{whole}$$

$$\text{whole} = 15\left(\frac{500}{3}\right) = 5(500) = 2{,}500$$

[handwritten notes:]
$$\text{Part} = \frac{1}{100} \times \text{whole}$$
$$15 = \frac{3}{5}\left(\frac{1}{100}\right) \times \text{whole}$$
$$15 = \frac{3}{500} \times \text{whole}$$
$$15 \times \frac{500}{3} = \text{whole}$$
$$2500 = \text{whole}$$

13. How to use the PERCENT INCREASE/DECREASE FORMULAS

Identify the original whole and the amount of increase/decrease.

$$\textit{Percent increase} = \frac{\textit{amount of increase}}{\textit{original whole}} \times 100\%$$

$$\textit{Percent decrease} = \frac{\textit{amount of decrease}}{\textit{original whole}} \times 100\%$$

Example: The price goes up from \$80 to \$100. What is the percent increase?

Setup: $\text{Percent increase} = \frac{20}{80} \times 100\% = 25\%$

14. How to predict whether a sum, difference, or product will be ODD or EVEN

Don't bother memorizing the rules. Just take simple numbers like 1 and 2 and see what happens.

Example: If m is even and n is odd, is the product mn odd or even?

Setup: Say $m = 2$ and $n = 1$.
2×1 is even, so mn is even.

15. How to recognize MULTIPLES OF 2, 3, 4, 5, 6, 9, 10, and 12

2: Last digit is even.

3: Sum of digits is a multiple of 3.

4: Last two digits are a multiple of 4.

5: Last digit is 5 or 0.

6: Sum of digits is a multiple of 3, and last digit is even.

9: Sum of digits is a multiple of 9.

10: Last digit is 0.

12: Sum of digits is a multiple of 3, and last two digits are a multiple of 4.

16. How to find a COMMON FACTOR

Break both numbers down to their prime factors to see what they have in common. Then multiply the shared prime factors to find all common factors.

Example: What factors greater than 1 do 135 and 225 have in common?

Setup: First find the prime factors of 135 and 225; $135 = 3 \times 3 \times 3 \times 5$, and $225 = 3 \times 3 \times 5 \times 5$. The numbers share $3 \times 3 \times 5$ in common. Thus, aside from 3 and 5, the remaining common factors can be found by multiplying 3, 3, and 5 in every possible combination: $3 \times 3 = 9$, $3 \times 5 = 15$, and $3 \times 3 \times 5 = 45$.

17. How to find a COMMON MULTIPLE

The product is the easiest common multiple to find. If the two numbers have any factors in common, you can divide them out of the product to get a lower common multiple.

Example: What is the least common multiple of 28 and 42?

Setup: The product of $28 \times 42 = 1,176$, a common multiple but not the least. However, $28 = 2 \times 2 \times 7$, and $42 = 2 \times 3 \times 7$. They share a 2 and a 7, so divide the product by 2 and then by 7: $1,176 \div 2 = 588$, and $588 \div 7 = 84$. The least common multiple is 84.

18. How to find the AVERAGE

$$Average = \frac{Sum\ of\ terms}{Number\ of\ terms}$$

Example: What is the average of 3, 4, and 8?

Setup: $Average = \frac{3+4+8}{3} = \frac{15}{3} = 5.$

19. How to use the AVERAGE to find the SUM

$$Sum = (Average) \times (Number\ of\ terms)$$

Example: 17.5 is the average (arithmetic mean) of 24 numbers. What is the sum?

Setup: Sum = 17.5 × 24 = 420

20. How to find the AVERAGE of CONSECUTIVE NUMBERS

The average of evenly spaced numbers is simply the average of the smallest number and the largest number. The average of all the integers from 13 to 77, for example, is the same as the average of 13 and 77:

$$\frac{13+77}{2} = \frac{90}{2} = 45$$

21. How to COUNT CONSECUTIVE NUMBERS

The number of integers from A to B inclusive is $B - A + 1$.

Example: How many integers are there from 73 through 419, inclusive?

Setup: 419 – 73 + 1 = 347

22. How to find the SUM OF CONSECUTIVE NUMBERS

$$Sum = (Average) \times (Number\ of\ terms)$$

Example: What is the sum of the integers from 10 through 50, inclusive?

Setup: Average = (10 + 50) ÷ 2 = 30
Number of terms = 50 – 10 + 1 = 41 Sum = 30 × 41 = 1,230

23. **How to find the MEDIAN**

Put the numbers in numerical order and take the middle number. (If there's an even number of numbers, the average of the two numbers in the middle is the median.)

Example: What is the median of 88, 86, 57, 94, and 73?

Setup: Put the numbers in numerical order and take the middle number:
57, 73, 86, 88, 94

The median is 86.

24. **How to find the MODE**

Take the number that appears most often. For example, if your test scores are 88, 57, 68, 85, 98, 93, 93, 84, and 81, the mode of the scores is 93 because it appears more often than any other score. (If there's a tie for most often, then there's more than one mode.)

25. **How to find the RANGE**

Simply take the positive difference between the highest and lowest values. Using the previous example, if your test scores are 88, 57, 68, 85, 98, 93, 93, 84, and 81, the range of the scores is 41, the highest value minus the lowest value (98 − 57 = 41).

26. **How to use actual numbers to determine a RATIO**

To find a ratio, put the number associated with *of* on the top and the word associated with *to* on the bottom.

$$Ratio = \frac{of}{to}$$

The ratio of 20 oranges to 12 apples is $\frac{20}{12}$, or $\frac{5}{3}$.

27. How to use a ratio to determine an ACTUAL NUMBER

Set up a proportion.

Example: The ratio of boys to girls is 3 to 4. If there are 135 boys, how many girls are there?

Setup: $\dfrac{3}{4} = \dfrac{135}{x}$

$3 \times x = 4 \times 135$

$x = 180$

28. How to use actual numbers to determine a RATE

Identify the quantities and the units to be compared. Keep the units straight.

Example: Anders typed 9,450 words in $3\frac{1}{2}$ hours.
What was his rate in words per minute?

Setup: First convert $3\frac{1}{2}$ hours to 210 minutes. Then set up the rate with words on top and minutes on bottom:

$\dfrac{9{,}450 \text{ words}}{210 \text{ minutes}} = 45$ words per minute

29. How to deal with TABLES, GRAPHS, AND CHARTS

Read the question and all labels extra carefully. Ignore extraneous information and zero in on what the question asks for. Take advantage of the spread in the answer choices by approximating the answer whenever possible.

30. **How to count the NUMBER OF POSSIBILITIES**

In most cases, you won't need to apply the combination and permutation formulas on the GRE. The number of possibilities is generally so small that the best approach is just to write them out systematically and count them.

Example: How many three-digit numbers can be formed with the digits 1, 3, and 5 used only once?

Setup: Write them out. Be systematic so you don't miss any: 135, 153, 315, 351, 513, 531. Count them: six possibilities.

31. **How to calculate a simple PROBABILITY**

$$Probability = \frac{Number\ of\ favorable\ outcomes}{Total\ number\ of\ possible\ outcomes}$$

Example: What is the probability of throwing a 5 on a fair six-sided die?

Setup: There is one favorable outcome—throwing a 5. There are 6 possible outcomes—one for each side of the die.

$$Probability = \frac{1}{6}$$

32. **How to work with new SYMBOLS**

If you see a symbol you've never seen before, don't freak out: it's a made-up symbol. Everything you need to know is in the question stem. Just follow the instructions.

33. **How to SIMPLIFY POLYNOMIALS**

First multiply to eliminate all parentheses. Each term inside one parentheses is multiplied by each term inside the other parentheses. All like terms are then combined.

Example: $(3x^2+5x)(x-1) =$
$3x^2(x-1) + 5x(x-1) =$
$3x^3 - 3x^2 + 5x^2 - 5x =$
$3x^3 + 2x^2 - 5x$

34. How to FACTOR certain POLYNOMIALS

Learn to spot these classic factorables:

$$ab + ac = a(b + c)$$

$$a^2 + 2ab + b^2 = (a + b)^2$$

$$a^2 - 2ab + b^2 = (a - b)^2$$

$$a^2 - b^2 = (a - b)(a + b)$$

35. How to solve for one variable IN TERMS OF ANOTHER

To find x "in terms of" y, isolate x on one side, leaving y as the only variable on the other.

36. How to solve an INEQUALITY

Treat it much like an equation—adding, subtracting, multiplying, and dividing both sides by the same thing. Just remember to reverse the inequality sign if you multiply or divide by a negative quantity.

Example: Rewrite $7 - 3x > 2$ in its simplest form.

Setup: $7 - 3x > 2$
Subtract 7 from both sides:
$7 - 3x - 7 > 2 - 7$
So $-3x > -5$. Now divide both sides by -3 and remember to reverse the inequality sign:

$$x < \frac{5}{3}$$

37. How to handle ABSOLUTE VALUES

The *absolute value* of a number n, denoted by $|n|$, is defined as n if $n \geq 0$ and $-n$ if $n < 0$. The absolute value of a number is the distance from zero to the number on the number line:

$$|-5| = 5$$

If $|x| = 3$, then x could be 3 or -3.

Example: If $|x - 3| < 2$, what is the range of possible values for x?

Setup: $|x - 3| < 2$, so $(x - 3) < 2$ and
$-(x - 3) < 2$
So $x - 3 < 2$ and $x - 3 > -2$
So $x < 2 + 3$ and $x > -2 + 3$
So $x < 5$ and $x > 1$
So $1 < x < 5$

38. How to TRANSLATE ENGLISH INTO ALGEBRA

Look for the key words and systematically turn phrases into algebraic expressions and sentences into equations.

Here's a table of key words that you may have to translate into mathematical terms:

Operation	Key Words
Addition	sum, plus, and, added to, more than, increased by, combined with, exceeds, total, greater than
Subtraction	difference between, minus, subtracted from, decreased by, diminished by, less than, reduced by
Multiplication	of, product, times, multiplied by, twice, double, triple, half
Division	quotient, divided by, per, out of, ratio of __ to __
Equals	equals, is, was, will be, the result is, adds up to, costs, is the same as

39. How to find an ANGLE formed by INTERSECTING LINES

Vertical angles are equal. Adjacent angles add up to 180°.

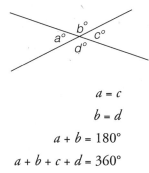

$$a = c$$
$$b = d$$
$$a + b = 180°$$
$$a + b + c + d = 360°$$

40. How to find an angle formed by a TRANSVERSAL across PARALLEL LINES

All the acute angles are equal. All the obtuse angles are equal. An acute plus an obtuse equals 180°.

Example:

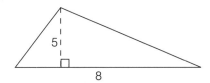

ℓ_1 is parallel to ℓ_2

$$e = g = p = r$$
$$f = h = q = s$$
$$e + q = g + s = 180°$$

41. How to find the AREA of a TRIANGLE

$$Area = \frac{1}{2}(base)(height)$$

Example:

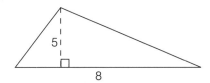

Setup: $Area = \dfrac{1}{2}(8)(5) = 20$

42. How to work with ISOSCELES TRIANGLES

Isosceles triangles have two equal sides and two equal angles. If a GRE question tells you that a triangle is isoceles, you can bet that you'll need to use that information to find the length of a side or a measure of an angle.

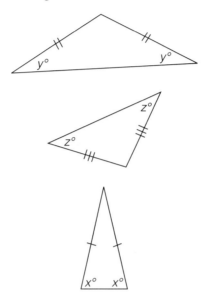

43. How to work with EQUILATERAL TRIANGLES

Equilateral triangles have three equal sides and three 60° angles. If a GRE question tells you that a triangle is equilateral, you can bet that you'll need to use that information to find the length of a side or a measure of an angle.

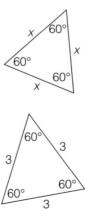

44. How to work with SIMILAR TRIANGLES

In similar triangles, corresponding angles are equal, and corresponding sides are proportional. If a GRE question tells you that triangles are similar, you'll probably need that information to find the length of a side or the measure of an angle.

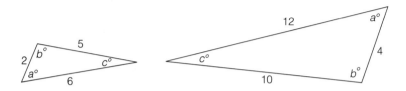

45. How to find the HYPOTENUSE or a LEG of a RIGHT TRIANGLE

Pythagorean theorem: $a^2 + b^2 = c^2$

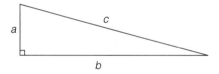

46. How to spot SPECIAL RIGHT TRIANGLES

3-4-5

5-12-13

30-60-90

45-45-90

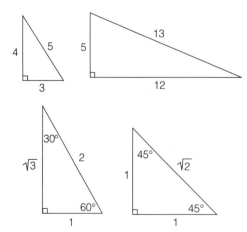

47. How to find the PERIMETER of a RECTANGLE

$$Perimeter = 2(length + width)$$

Example:

Setup: Perimeter = 2(2 + 5) = 14

48. How to find the AREA of a RECTANGLE

$$Area = (length)(width)$$

Example:

Setup: Area = 2 × 5 = 10

49. How to find the AREA of a SQUARE

$$Area = (side)^2$$

Example:

Setup: Area = 3^2 = 9

50. How to find the AREA of a PARALLELOGRAM

Area = (*base*)(*height*)

Example:

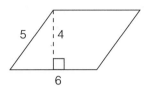

Setup: Area = 6 × 4 = 24

51. How to find the AREA of a TRAPEZOID

A trapezoid is a quadrilateral having only two parallel sides. You can always drop a line or two to break the figure into a rectangle and a triangle or two triangles. Use the area formulas for those familiar shapes. You could also apply the general formula for the area of a trapezoid:

Area = (*average of parallel sides*) × (*height*)

Example:

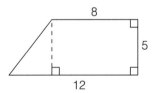

Setup: Area of rectangle = 8 × 5 = 40

Area of triangle = $\frac{1}{2}(4 \times 5) = 10$

Area of trapezoid = 40 + 10 = 50

52. How to find the CIRCUMFERENCE of a CIRCLE

$$Circumference = 2\pi r$$

Example:

Setup: Circumference = $2\pi(5) = 10\pi$

53. How to find the AREA of a CIRCLE

$$Area = \pi r^2$$

Example:

Setup: Area = $\pi \times 5^2 = 25\pi$

54. How to find the DISTANCE BETWEEN POINTS on the coordinate plane

If two points have the same x's or the same y's—that is, they make a line segment that is parallel to an axis—all you have to do is subtract the numbers that are different.

Example: What is the distance from (2, 3) to (–7, 3)?

Setup: The y's are the same, so just subtract the x's: 2 –(–7) = 9

If the points have different x's and different y's, make a right triangle and use the Pythagorean theorem.

Example: What is the distance from (2, 3) to (–1, –1)?

Setup:

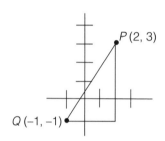

It's a 3-4-5 triangle!
$PQ = 5$

55. How to find the SLOPE of a LINE

$$Slope = \frac{rise}{run} = \frac{change\ in\ y}{change\ in\ x}$$

Example: What is the slope of the line that contains the points (1, 2) and (4, –5)?

Setup: $Slope = \dfrac{-5-2}{4-1} = \dfrac{-7}{3}$

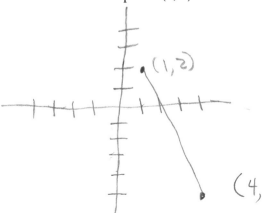

LEVEL 3 (Math You Might Find Difficult)

56. How to determine COMBINED PERCENT INCREASE/DECREASE

Start with 100 and see what happens.

Example: A price rises by 10 percent one year and by 20 percent the next. What's the combined percent increase?

Setup: Say the original price is $100.

Year one:
$100 + (10% of 100) =
100 + 10 = 110

Year two:
110 + (20% of 110) =
110 + 22 = 132

From 100 to 132—that's a 32 percent increase.

57. How to find the ORIGINAL WHOLE before percent increase/decrease

Think of a 15 percent increase over x as $1.15x$ and set up an equation.

Example: After decreasing by 5 percent, the population is now 57,000. What was the original population?

Setup: $0.95 \times$ (Original Population) = 57,000
Original Population =
$57,000 \div 0.95 = 60,000$

58. How to solve a SIMPLE INTEREST problem

With simple interest, the interest is computed on the principal only using the following formula:

$$interest = (principal) \times (interest\ rate\text{*}) \times (time\text{**})$$

* expressed as a decimal

** expressed in years

Example: If $12,000 is invested at 6 percent simple annual interest, how much interest is earned after 9 months?

Setup: $(12,000) \times (0.06) \times \left(\dfrac{9}{12}\right) = \$540$

59. How to solve a COMPOUND INTEREST problem

If interest is compounded, the interest is computed on the principal as well as on any interest earned. To compute compound interest:

$$(final\ balance) = (principal) \times \left(1 + \frac{interest\ rate}{C}\right)^{(time)(C)}$$

where C = the number of times compounded annually

Example: If $10,000 is invested at 8 percent annual interest, compounded semiannually, what is the balance after 1 year?

Setup: Final balance

$$= (10,000) \times \left(1 + \frac{0.08}{2}\right)^{(1)(2)}$$

$$= (10,000) \times (1.04)^2$$

$$= \$10,816$$

60. How to solve a REMAINDERS problem

Pick a number that fits the given conditions and see what happens.

Example: When n is divided by 7, the remainder is 5. What is the remainder when $2n$ is divided by 7?

Setup: Find a number that leaves a remainder of 5 when divided by 7. A good choice would be 12. If $n = 12$, then $2n = 24$, which, when divided by 7, leaves a remainder of 3.

61. How to solve a DIGITS problem

Use a little logic—and some trial and error.

Example: If A, B, C, and D represent distinct digits in the addition problem below, what is the value of D?

$$\begin{array}{r} AB \\ +\,BA \\ \hline CDC \end{array}$$

Setup: Two 2-digit numbers will add up to at most something in the 100s, so $C = 1$. B plus A in the units' column gives a 1, and since it can't simply be that $B + A = 1$, it must be that $B + A = 11$, and a 1 gets carried. In fact, A and B can be any pair of digits that add up to 11 (3 and 8, 4 and 7, etc.), but it doesn't matter what they are—they always give you the same thing for D:

$$\begin{array}{r} 47 \\ +74 \\ \hline 121 \end{array} \qquad \begin{array}{r} 83 \\ +38 \\ \hline 121 \end{array}$$

62. **How to find a WEIGHTED AVERAGE**

Give each term the appropriate "weight."

Example: The girls' average score is 30. The boys' average score is 24. If there are twice as many boys as girls, what is the overall average?

Setup:
$$\text{Weighted Avg.} = \frac{1 \times 30 + 2 \times 24}{3} = \frac{78}{3} = 26$$

HINT: Don't just average the averages.

63. **How to find the NEW AVERAGE when a number is added or deleted**

Use the sum of the terms of the old average to help you find the new average.

Example: Michael's average score after four tests is 80. If he scores 100 on the fifth test, what's his new average?

Setup: Find the original sum from the original average:

Original sum = 4 × 80 = 320

Add the fifth score to make the new sum:

New sum = 320 + 100 = 420

Find the new average from the new sum:

$$\text{New average} = \frac{420}{5} = 84$$

64. **How to use the ORIGINAL AVERAGE and NEW AVERAGE to figure out WHAT WAS ADDED OR DELETED**

Use the sums.

Number added = (new sum) – (original sum)

Number deleted = (original sum) – (new sum)

Example: The average of five numbers is 2. After one number is deleted, the new average is –3. What number was deleted?

Setup: Find the original sum from the original average:

Original sum = 5 × 2 = 10

Find the new sum from the new average:

New sum = 4 × (–3) = –12

The difference between the original sum and the new sum is the answer.

Number deleted = 10 – (–12) = 22

65. How to find an AVERAGE RATE

Convert to totals.

$$Average\ A\ per\ B = \frac{Total\ A}{Total\ B}$$

Example: If the first 500 pages have an average of 150 words per page, and the remaining 100 pages have an average of 450 words per page, what is the average number of words per page for the entire 600 pages?

Setup: Total pages = 500 + 100 = 600
Total words = 500 × 150 + 100 × 450 = 120,000

$$Average\ words\ per\ page = \frac{120,000}{600} = 200$$

To find an average speed, you also convert to totals.

$$Average\ speed = \frac{Total\ distance}{Time}$$

Example: Rosa drove 120 miles one way at an average speed of 40 miles per hour and returned by the same 120-mile route at an average speed of 60 miles per hour. What was Rosa's average speed for the entire 240-mile round trip?

Setup: To drive 120 miles at 40 mph takes 3 hours. To return at 60 mph takes 2 hours. The total time, then, is 5 hours.

$$Average\ speed = \frac{240\ miles}{5\ hours} = 48\ mph$$

66. How to solve a WORK PROBLEM

In a work problem, you are given the rate at which people or machines perform work individually and asked to compute the rate at which they work together (or vice versa). The work formula: The inverse of the time it would take everyone working together equals the sum of the inverses of the times it would take each working individually. In other words,

$$\frac{1}{r} + \frac{1}{s} = \frac{1}{t}$$

where r and s are, for example, the number of hours it would take Rebecca and Sam, respectively to complete a job working by themselves and t is the number of hours it would take the two of them working together.

Example: If it takes Joe 4 hours to paint a room and Pete twice as long to paint the same room, how long would it take the two of them, working together, to paint the same room, if each of them works at his respective individual rate?

Setup: Joe takes 4 hours, so Pete takes 8 hours. Thus,

$$\frac{1}{4} + \frac{1}{8} = \frac{1}{t}$$

$$\frac{2}{8} + \frac{1}{8} = \frac{1}{t}$$

$$\frac{3}{8} = \frac{1}{t}$$

$$t = \frac{1}{\left(\frac{3}{8}\right)} = \frac{8}{3}$$

So it would take them $\frac{8}{3}$ hours, or 2 hours 40 minutes, to paint the room together.

67. **How to determine a COMBINED RATIO**

Multiply one or both ratios by whatever you need to in order to get the terms they have in common to match.

Example: The ratio of a to b is 7:3. The ratio of b to c is 2:5. What is the ratio of a to c ?

Setup: Multiply each member of a: b by 2 and multiply each member of b: c by 3, and you get a: b = 14:6 and b: c = 6:15. Now that the b's match, you can just take a and c and say a: c = 14:15.

68. **How to solve a DILUTION or MIXTURE problem**

In dilution or mixture problems, you have to determine the characteristics of the resulting mixture when substances with different characteristics are combined. Or, alternatively, you have to determine how to combine substances with different characteristics to produce a desired mixture. There are two approaches to such problems—the straightforward setup and the balancing method.

Example: If 5 pounds of raisins that cost $1 per pound are mixed with 2 pounds of almonds that cost $2.40 per pound, what is the cost per pound of the resulting mixture?

Setup: The straightforward setup:

($1)(5) + ($2.40)(2) = $9.80

The cost per pound is $n = \$\dfrac{9.80}{7} = \$1.40$

Example: How many liters of a solution that is 10 percent alcohol by volume must be added to 2 liters of a solution that is 50 percent alcohol by volume to create a solution that is 15 percent alcohol by volume?

Setup: The balancing method: Make the weaker and stronger (or cheaper and more expensive, etc.) substances balance. That is, (percent/price difference between the weaker solution and the desired solution) × (amount of weaker solution) = (percent/price difference between the stronger solution and the desired solution) × (amount of stronger solution).

In this case: $n(15 - 10) = 2(50 - 15)$

$$n \times 5 = 2(35)$$

$$n = \frac{70}{5} = 14$$

So 14 liters of the 10 percent solution must be added.

69. How to solve a GROUP problem involving BOTH/NEITHER

Some GRE word problems involve two groups with overlapping members and possibly elements that belong to neither group. It's easy to identify this type of question because the words *both* and/or *neither* appear in the question. These problems are quite easy if you memorize the following formula:

Group 1 + Group 2 + Neither − Both = Total

Example: Of the 120 students at a certain language school, 65 are studying French, 51 are studying Spanish, and 53 are studying neither language. How many are studying both French and Spanish?

Setup: $65 + 51 + 53 - \text{Both} = 120$

$$169 - \text{Both} = 120$$

$$\text{Both} = 49$$

70. How to solve a GROUP problem involving EITHER/OR CATEGORIES

Other GRE word problems involve groups with distinct "either/or" categories (male/female, blue-collar/white-collar, etc.). The key to solving this type of problem is to organize the information in a grid.

Example: At a certain professional conference with 130 attendees, 94 of the attendees are doctors, and the rest are dentists. If 48 of the attendees are women and $\frac{1}{4}$ of the dentists in attendance are women, how many of the attendees are male doctors?

Setup: To complete the grid, each row and column adds up to the corresponding total:

	Doctors	Dentists	Total
Male	55	27	82
Female	39	9	48
Total	94	36	130

After you've filled in the information from the question, simply fill in the remaining boxes until you get the number you are looking for—in this case, that 55 of the attendees are male doctors.

71. How to work with FACTORIALS

You may see a problem involving factorial notation. If n is an integer greater than 1, then n factorial, denoted by $n!$, is defined as the product of all the integers from 1 to n. In other words:

$$2! = 2 \times 1 = 2$$
$$3! = 3 \times 2 \times 1 = 6$$
$$4! = 4 \times 3 \times 2 \times 1 = 24, \text{ etc.}$$

By definition, $0! = 1! = 1$.

Also note: $6! = 6 \times 5! = 6 \times 5 \times 4!$, etc. Most GRE factorial problems test your ability to factor and/or cancel.

Example: $\dfrac{8!}{6! \times 2!} = \dfrac{8 \times 7 \times 6!}{6! \times 2 \times 1} = 28$

72. How to solve a PERMUTATION problem

Factorials are useful for solving questions about permutations (i.e., the number of ways to arrange elements sequentially). For instance, to figure out how many ways there are to arrange 7 items along a shelf, you would multiply the number of possibilities for the first position times the number of possibilities remaining for the second position, and so on—in other words: $7 \times 6 \times 5 \times 4 \times 3 \times 2 \times 1$, or $7!$.

If you're asked to find the number of ways to arrange a smaller group that's being drawn from a larger group, you can either apply logic, or you can use the permutation formula:

$$_nP_k = \frac{n!}{(n-k)!}$$

where n = (# in the larger group) and k = (# you're arranging).

Example: Five runners run in a race. The runners who come in first, second, and third place will win gold, silver, and bronze medals respectively. How many possible outcomes for gold, silver, and bronze medal winners are there?

Setup: Any of the 5 runners could come in first place, leaving 4 runners who could come in second place, leaving 3 runners who could come in third place, for a total of $5 \times 4 \times 3 = 60$ possible outcomes for gold, silver, and bronze medal winners. Or, using the formula:

$$_5P_3 = \frac{5!}{(5-3)!} = \frac{5!}{2!} = 5 \times 4 \times 3 = 60$$

73. How to solve a COMBINATION problem

If the order or arrangement of the smaller group that's being drawn from the larger group does NOT matter, you are looking for the numbers of combinations, and a different formula is called for:

$$_nC_k \frac{n!}{k!(n-k)!}$$

Where n = (# in the larger group) and k = (# you're choosing)

Example: How many different ways are there to choose 3 delegates from 8 possible candidates?

Setup: $_8C_3 = \dfrac{8!}{3! \times 5!} = \dfrac{8 \times 7 \times 6 \times 5!}{3 \times 2 \times 1 \times 5!} = 56$

So there are 56 different possible combinations.

74. How to solve PROBABILITY problems where probabilities must be multiplied

Suppose that a random process is performed. Then there is a set of possible outcomes that can occur. An event is a set of possible outcomes. We are concerned with the probability of events.

When all the outcomes are equally likely, the basic probability formula is this:

$$Probability = \frac{Number\ of\ desired\ outcomes}{Number\ of\ possible\ outcomes}$$

Many hard probability questions involve finding the probability that several events occur. Let's consider first the case of the probability that two events occur. Call these two events A and B.

The probability that both events occur is the probability that event A occurs multiplied by the probability that event B occurs given that event A occurred. The probability that B occurs given that A occurs is called the conditional probability that B occurs given that A occurs. Except when events A and B do not depend on one another, the probability that B occurs given that A occurs is not the same as the probability that B occurs.

The probability that three events A, B, and C occur is the probability that A occurs multiplied by the conditional probability that B occurs given that A occurred multiplied by the conditional probability that C occurs given that both A and B have occurred.

This can be generalized to n events, where n is a positive integer greater than 3.

Example: If 2 students are chosen at random to run an errand from a class with 5 girls and 5 boys, what is the probability that both students chosen will be girls?

Setup: The probability that the first student chosen will be a girl is $\dfrac{5}{10} = \dfrac{1}{2}$, and since there would be 4 girls and 5 boys left out of 9 students, the probability that the second student chosen will be a girl (given that the first student chosen is a girl) is $\dfrac{4}{9}$. Thus, the probability that both students chosen will be girls is $\dfrac{1}{2} \times \dfrac{4}{9} = \dfrac{2}{9}$.

Let's consider another example where a random process is repeated.

Example: If a fair coin is tossed 4 times, what's the probability that at least 3 of the 4 tosses will be heads?

Setup: There are 2 possible outcomes for each toss, so after 4 tosses, there are $2 \times 2 \times 2 \times 2 = 16$ possible outcomes.

We can list the different possible sequences where at least 3 of the 4 tosses are heads. These sequences are

HHHT
HHTH
HTHH
THHH
HHHH

Thus, the probability that at least 3 of the 4 tosses will come up heads is:

$$\frac{\text{Number of favorable outcomes}}{\text{Number of possible outcomes}} = \frac{5}{16}$$

We could have also solved this question using the combinations formula.

The probability of a head is $\dfrac{1}{2}$ and the probability of a tail is $\dfrac{1}{2}$. The probability of any particular sequence of heads and tails resulting from 4 tosses is $\dfrac{1}{2} \times \dfrac{1}{2} \times \dfrac{1}{2} \times \dfrac{1}{2}$, which is $\dfrac{1}{16}$.

Suppose that the result each of the four tosses is recorded in each of the four spaces.

———   ———   ———   ———

Thus, we would record an H for head or a T for tails in each of the 4 spaces.

The number of ways of having exactly 3 heads among the 4 tosses is the number of ways of choosing 3 of the 4 spaces above to record an H for heads.

The number of ways of choosing 3 of the 4 spaces is

$$_4C_3 = \frac{4!}{3!(4-3)!} = \frac{4!}{3!(1)!} = \frac{4 \times 3 \times 2 \times 1}{3 \times 2 \times 1 \times 1} = 4.$$

The number of ways of having exactly 4 heads among the 4 tosses is 1.

If we use the combinations formula, using the definition that $0! = 1$, then

$$_4C_4 = \frac{4!}{4!(4-4)!} = \frac{4!}{4!(0)!} = \frac{4!}{4!(0)!}$$

$$= \frac{4 \times 3 \times 2 \times 1}{4 \times 3 \times 2 \times 1 \times 1} = 1.$$

Thus, $_4C_3 = 4$ and $_4C_4 = 1$. So the number of different sequences containing at least 3 heads is $4 + 1 = 5$.

The probability of having at least 3 heads is $\frac{5}{16}$.

75. How to deal with STANDARD DEVIATION

Like mean, mode, median, and range, standard deviation is a term used to describe sets of numbers. Standard deviation is a measure of how spread out a set of numbers is (how much the numbers deviate from the mean). The greater the spread, the higher the standard deviation. You'll never actually have to calculate the standard deviation on Test Day, but here's how it's calculated:

• Find the average (arithmetic mean) of the set.

• Find the differences between the mean and each value in the set.

• Square each of the differences.

- Find the average of the squared differences.

- Take the positive square root of the average.

Although you won't have to calculate standard deviation on the GRE, you may be asked to compare standard deviations between sets of data or otherwise demonstrate that you understand what standard deviation means.

Example: High temperatures, in degrees Fahrenheit, in 2 cities over 5 days:

September	1	2	3	4	5
City A	54	61	70	49	56
City B	62	56	60	67	65

For the 5-day period listed, which city had the greater standard deviation in high temperatures?

Setup: Even without trying to calculate them out, one can see that City A has the greater spread in temperatures and, therefore, the greater standard deviation in high temperatures. If you were to go ahead and calculate the standard deviations following the steps described above, you would find that the standard deviation in

high temperatures for City $A = \sqrt{\frac{254}{5}} \approx 7.1$,

while the standard deviation for City $B = \sqrt{\frac{74}{5}} \approx 3.8$.

76. How to MULTIPLY/DIVIDE POWERS

Add/subtract the exponents.

Example: $x^a \times x^b = x^{a+b}$
$2^3 \times 2^4 = 2^7$

Example: $\frac{x^c}{x^d} = x^{c-d}$

$\frac{5^6}{5^2} = 5^4$

77. How to RAISE A POWER TO A POWER TO AN EXPONENT

Multiply the exponents.

Example: $(x^a)^b = x^{ab}$
$(3^4)^5 = 3^{20}$

78. How to handle POWERS with a base of ZERO and POWERS with an EXPONENT of ZERO

Zero raised to any nonzero exponent equals zero.

Example: $0^4 = 0^{12} = 0^1 = 0$

Any nonzero number raised to the exponent 0 equals 1.

Example: $3^0 = 15^0 = (0.34)^0 = -345^0 = \pi^0 = 1$

The lone exception is 0 raised to the 0 power, which is *undefined*.

79. How to handle NEGATIVE POWERS

A number raised to the exponent $-x$ is the reciprocal of that number raised to the exponent x.

Example: $5^{-3} = \dfrac{1}{5^3} = \dfrac{1}{5 \times 5 \times 5} = \dfrac{1}{125}$

$n^{-1} = \dfrac{1}{n}, n^{-2} = \dfrac{1}{n^2}$, and so on.

80. How to handle FRACTIONAL POWERS

Fractional exponents relate to roots. For instance, $x^{\frac{1}{2}} = \sqrt{x}$.

Likewise, $x^{\frac{1}{3}} = \sqrt[3]{x}, x^{\frac{2}{3}} = \sqrt[3]{x^2}$, and so on.

Example: $4^{\frac{1}{2}} = \sqrt{4} = 2$

$(x^{-2})^{\frac{1}{2}} = x^{(-2)\left(\frac{1}{2}\right)} = x^{-1} = \dfrac{1}{x}$

81. How to handle CUBE ROOTS

The cube root of x is just the number that multiplied by itself 3 times (i.e., cubed) gives you x. Both positive and negative numbers have one and only one cube root, denoted by the symbol $\sqrt{3}$, and the cube root of a number is always the same sign as the number itself.

Example: $(-5) \times (-5) \times (-5) = -125$, so $\sqrt[3]{-125}$

$$= -5$$

$$\frac{1}{2} \times \frac{1}{2} \times \frac{1}{2} = \frac{1}{8}, \text{ so } \sqrt[3]{\frac{1}{8}} = \frac{1}{2}$$

82. How to ADD, SUBTRACT, MULTIPLY, and DIVIDE ROOTS

You can add/subtract roots only when the parts inside the $\sqrt{}$ are identical.

Example: $\sqrt{2} + 3\sqrt{2} = 4\sqrt{2}$

$$\sqrt{2} - 3\sqrt{2} = -2\sqrt{2}$$

$\sqrt{2} + \sqrt{3}$ cannot be combined.

To multiply/divide roots, deal with what's inside the $\sqrt{}$ and outside the $\sqrt{}$ separately.

Example: $(2\sqrt{3})(7\sqrt{5}) = (2 \times 7)(\sqrt{3 \times 5}) = 14\sqrt{15}$

$$\frac{10\sqrt{21}}{5\sqrt{3}} = \frac{10}{5}\sqrt{\frac{21}{3}} = 2\sqrt{7}$$

83. How to SIMPLIFY A RADICAL

Look for perfect squares (4, 9, 16, 25, 36,...) inside the $\sqrt{}$. Factor them out and "unsquare" them.

Example: $\sqrt{48} = \sqrt{16} \times \sqrt{3} = 4\sqrt{3}$

$$\sqrt{180} = \sqrt{36} \times \sqrt{5} = 6\sqrt{5}$$

84. How to solve certain QUADRATIC EQUATIONS

Forget the quadratic formula. Manipulate the equation (if necessary) into the "_____ = 0" form, factor the left side, and break the quadratic into two simple equations.

Example:
$$x^2 + 6 = 5x$$
$$x^2 - 5x + 6 = 0$$
$$(x - 2)(x - 3) = 0$$
$$x - 2 = 0 \text{ or } x - 3 = 0$$
$$x = 2 \text{ or } 3$$

Example:
$$x^2 = 9$$
$$x = 3 \text{ or } -3$$

85. How to solve MULTIPLE EQUATIONS

When you see two equations with two variables on the GRE, they're probably easy to combine in such a way that you get something closer to what you're looking for.

Example: If $5x - 2y = -9$ and $3y - 4x = 6$, what is the value of $x + y$?

Setup: The question doesn't ask for x and y separately, so don't solve for them separately if you don't have to. Look what happens if you just rearrange a little and "add" the equations:

$$
\begin{array}{r}
5x - 2y = -9 \\
\underline{-4x + 3y = \ 6} \\
x + y = -3
\end{array}
$$

86. How to solve a SEQUENCE problem

The notation used in sequence problems scares many test takers, but these problems aren't as bad as they look. In a sequence problem, the nth term in the sequence is generated by performing an operation, which will be defined for you, on either n or on the previous term in the sequence. Familiarize yourself with sequence notation, and you should have no problem.

Example: What is the positive difference between the fifth and fourth terms in the sequence 0, 4, 18, … whose nth term is $n^2(n-1)$?

Setup: Use the operation given to come up with the values for your terms:

$$n_5 = 5^2(5-1) = 25(4) = 100$$
$$n_4 = 4^2(4-1) = 16(3) = 48$$

So the positive difference between the fifth and fourth terms is $100 - 48 = 52$.

87. How to solve a FUNCTION problem

You may see classic function notation on the GRE. An algebraic expression of only one variable may be defined as a function, f or g, of that variable.

Example: What is the minimum value of the function $f(x) = x^2 - 1$?

Setup: In the function $f(x) = x^2 - 1$, if x is 1, then $f(1) = 1^2 - 1 = 0$. In other words, by inputting 1 into the function, the output $f(x) = 0$. Every number inputted has one and only one output (although the reverse is not necessarily true). You're asked to find the minimum value, so how would you minimize the expression $f(x) = x^2 - 1$? Since x^2 cannot be negative, in this case $f(x)$ is minimized by making $x = 0$: $f(0) = 0^2 - 1 = -1$, so the minimum value of the function is -1.

88. How to handle GRAPHS of FUNCTIONS

You may see a problem that involves a function graphed onto the *xy*-coordinate plane, often called a "rectangular coordinate system" on the GRE. When graphing a function, the output, $f(x)$, becomes the *y*-coordinate. For example, in the previous example, $f(x) = x^2 - 1$, you've already determined 2 points, (1, 0) and (0, –1). If you were to keep plugging in numbers to determine more points and then plotted those points on the *xy*-coordinate plane, you would come up with something like this:

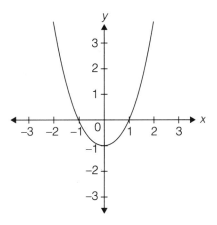

This curved line is called a *parabola*. In the event that you should see a parabola on the GRE (it could be upside down or more narrow or wider than the one shown), you will most likely be asked to choose which equation the parabola is describing. These questions can be surprisingly easy to answer. Pick out obvious points on the graph, such as (1, 0) and (0, –1) above, plug these values into the answer choices, and eliminate answer choices that don't jibe with those values until only one answer choice is left.

89. How to handle LINEAR EQUATIONS

You may also encounter linear equations on the GRE. A linear equation is often expressed in the form

$y = mx + b$, where

m = the slope of the line = $\dfrac{rise}{run}$

b = the y-intercept (where the line passes the y-axis).

For instance, a slope of 3 means that the line rises 3 steps for every 1 step it makes to the right. A positive slope slopes up from left to right. A negative slope slopes down from left to right. A slope of zero (e.g., $y = 5$) is a flat line.

Example: The graph of the linear equation

$y = -\dfrac{3}{4}x + 3$ is

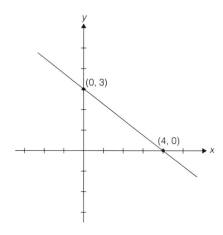

Note: The equation above could also be written in the form $3x + 4y = 12$.

To get a better handle on an equation written in this form, you can solve for y to write it in its more familiar form. Or, if you're asked to choose which equation the line is describing, you can pick obvious points such as (0, 3) and (4, 0) above and use these values to eliminate answer choices until only one answer is left.

90. **How to find the *x*- and *y*-INTERCEPTS of a line**

    The *x*-intercept of a line is the value of *x* where the line crosses the *x*-axis. In other words, it's the value of *x* when *y* = 0. Likewise, the *y*-intercept is the value of *y* where the line crosses the *y*-axis, or the value of *y* when *x* = 0. The *y*-intercept is also the value *b* when the equation is in the form *y* = *mx* + *b*. For instance, in the line shown in the previous example, the *x*-intercept is 4, and the *y*-intercept is 3.

91. **How to find the MAXIMUM and MINIMUM lengths for a SIDE of a TRIANGLE**

    If you know *n* = the lengths of two sides of a triangle, you know that the third side is between the positive difference and the sum.

    Example: The length of one side of a triangle is 7. The length of another side is 3. What is the range of possible lengths for the third side?

    Setup: The third side is greater than the difference (7 – 3 = 4) and less than the sum (7 + 3 = 10).

92. **How to find one angle or the sum of all the ANGLES of a REGULAR POLYGON**

    Sum of the interior angles in a polygon with *n* sides =

    $(n - 2) \times 180$

    Degree measure of one angle in a regular polygon with

    $n \text{ sides} = \dfrac{(n - 2) \times 180}{n}.$

    Example: What is the measure of one angle of a regular pentagon?

    Setup: Plug *n* = 5 into the formula:

    Degree measure of one angle =

    $\dfrac{(5 - 2) \times 180}{5} = \dfrac{540}{5} = 108$

93. How to find the LENGTH of an ARC

Think of an arc as a fraction of the circle's circumference.

$$\text{Length of } arc = \frac{n}{360} \times 2\pi r$$

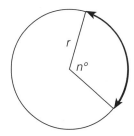

94. How to find the AREA of a SECTOR

Think of a sector as a fraction of the circle's area.

$$\text{Area of } sector = \frac{n}{360} \times \pi r^2$$

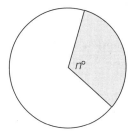

95. How to find the dimensions or area of an INSCRIBED or CIRCUMSCRIBED FIGURE

Look for the connection. Is the diameter the same as a side or a diagonal?

Example: If the area of the square is 36, what is the circumference of the circle?

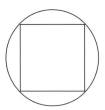

Setup: To get the circumference, you need the diameter or radius. The circle's diameter is also the square's diagonal, which (the diagonal creates two 45-45-90 triangles!) is $6\sqrt{2}$.

Circumference = π(diameter) = $6\pi\sqrt{2}$

96. How to find the VOLUME of a RECTANGULAR SOLID

Volume = length × width × height

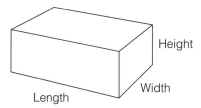

97. How to find the SURFACE AREA of a RECTANGULAR SOLID

To find the surface area of a rectangular solid, you have to find the area of each face and add them together. Here's the formula:

Surface area = 2(length × width + length × height + width × height)

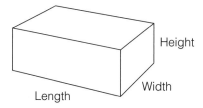

98. How to find the DIAGONAL of a RECTANGULAR SOLID

Use the Pythagorean theorem twice, unless you spot "special" triangles.

Example: What is the length of *AG*?

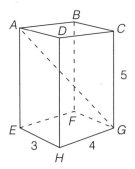

Setup: Draw diagonal *AC*.

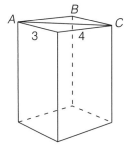

ABC is a 3-4-5 triangle, so *AC* = 5. Now look at triangle *ACG*:

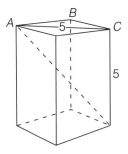

ACG is another special triangle, so you don't need to use the Pythagorean theorem. *ACG* is a 45-45-90, so *AG* = $5\sqrt{2}$.

99. How to find the VOLUME of a CYLINDER

Volume $= \pi r^2 h$

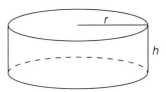

100. How to find the VOLUME of a SPHERE

Volume $= \dfrac{4}{3}\pi r^3$